PENGU

RANDOM

Hattie Hayridge was be ... ...tskirts of North London, on the cus... ...any secretarial jobs, her first stand-up com... ...erged in 1986 and she has since appeared on va... ...v shows, including *Red Dwarf*. In her early teens, her ambitions were to go to Africa, to do a parachute jump and to have her name on the front of a book. This is her first autobiography.

HATTIE HAYRIDGE

———

RANDOM ABSTRACT MEMORY

PENGUIN BOOKS

PENGUIN BOOKS

Published by the Penguin Group
Penguin Books Ltd, 27 Wrights Lane, London w8 5tz, England
Penguin Books USA Inc., 375 Hudson Street, New York, New York 10014, USA
Penguin Books Australia Ltd, Ringwood, Victoria, Australia
Penguin Books Canada Ltd, 10 Alcorn Avenue, Toronto, Ontario, Canada m4v 3b2
Penguin Books (NZ) Ltd, 182–190 Wairau Road, Auckland 10, New Zealand

Penguin Books Ltd, Registered Offices: Harmondsworth, Middlesex, England

First published 1997
1 3 5 7 9 10 8 6 4 2

Set in 10.5/14pt Monotype Bembo
Typeset by Rowland Phototypesetting Ltd, Bury St Edmunds, Suffolk
Printed in England by Clays Ltd, St Ives plc

For Mum and Dad

Acknowledgements

With thanks to: Monty, Dawn, Gretta, Linda, Rob, Gill, Flavia, Fiona, Chris, John, Beth, Lee, Jack, *The Landworker*, Do-Not-Press, Grant Naylor and Penguin.

Prologue

My birth sign is Sagittarius with a Cancer ascendant, which, if you believe in that sort of thing, means I am courageous but timid, extrovert but introvert, impatient but patient, adventurous but home-loving, passionate but cold, and half horse half crab.

When I was just a little girl my mother used to sing to me the Doris Day song, 'Que Sera, Sera (Whatever Will Be, Will Be)'. Sometimes I wish I could have been brought up with the sound of a less fatalistic song in my head; like 'Born to be Wild'.

I don't think I'm alone in that feeling.

1. *Appendix*

appendix *n.* an unnecessary bit of the gut, which would be useful if we ate grass.
baby *n.* a cute, gurgly little thing.

In those moments when we ruminate on the meaning of life, contemplate existence, speculate on predetermination, or just look up words in a thesaurus, I know I can only be grateful that I turned out to be one of these things and not the other.

Like many people born in the years B C (Before Camcorders), the events of my birth were not caught shakily in Technicolor on Hi-8 film with accompanying commentary. There was no fly-on-the-wall film crew, no candid or security cameras, and no maternity-ward artist in residence. We had to rely on the verbal scraps handed down to us by those in the know.

I was an only child. I still am. I'm sure my parents wanted children, but in those days the whole business was left in the laps of the Gods. I used to ask my mum why I didn't have any brothers and sisters and, after years of persistence, I finally dragged the truth out of her.

'I was too busy making your dad's sandwiches,' she told me, and if that's what my mum said, then that was good enough for me.

My parents were in their mid forties when I was born.

My mother had a good pregnancy, in the sense that she didn't know she was pregnant until the day I arrived. People have often commented, 'She *must* have known. You know, as a *woman*,' giving me a knowing look. 'You know, *things*, women's things, *you* know,' they'd say, delicately pointing downwards and wrinkling up their noses.

She had gone to the doctor when she thought she might be pregnant, but he'd told her, 'Don't be stupid, not at your age, it's just the change of life.' He was a doctor; he was an expert on the workings of the human body; he was in authority, therefore he must know what he was talking about. His vast knowledge and open mind, combined with a wealth of charm, tact and a warm bedside manner, meant that my mother didn't go back to see him again.

Life for the next few months carried on as normal for Mum. (I should by rights call her by her name, Lil, at this point, because she would not have answered at that time to the title 'Mum'.) She continued going out ballroom dancing and working as a cleaner in the Coach and Horses. This Hertfordshire pub was a couple of doors away from the two-up, two-down terraced house where she was brought up with her five brothers and sisters. Half a mile away was a similar terraced house where she now lived with her husband, Fred, or 'Dad' as he was yet to be known. They had been married for seventeen years. Fred had been born about a mile in the other direction, and he too had five brothers and sisters. There had been more babies, on both sides, but these had not survived childhood illness. Here, in this small town in Lea Valley, Hertfordshire/Essex border country, was the home where the sandwiches were

4

made. Every day, Fred would put the silver-foiled lunch-pack into his saddle-bag, and cycle the five miles uphill to the nursery, where he worked growing cucumbers.

One night, a week before Christmas, Lil couldn't sleep because of a pain she'd never had before. Never one to whinge about a little thing like suffering, she decided to wait and see if she felt better in the morning. Like most people they knew, Lil and Fred weren't on the phone. The plan was that Fred would call in at the surgery on his way to work, and ask the doctor to pop round. Lil, meanwhile, cleaned the outside of the front windows, both upstairs and downstairs, to give her something else to think about. The doctor arrived after his morning surgery, and after lunch. Since Lil opened the door to him, I suppose he thought it couldn't be that serious.

'Home visits are for people who can't get down to the surgery,' he said grudgingly. He walked into the living room. 'I suppose I'd better examine you now I'm here,' he continued in the same vein. 'It could be appendicitis.'

If I had a better memory, I might have been able to give my own account, because by now I could probably have got a good look at the doctor myself.

'I'm going to have to call an ambulance,' he told Lil. 'I think you're having contractions.'

With that, Lil still not knowing what was wrong with her, the ambulance was called and she was rushed to hospital.

She walked into the vehicle at home, and walked out of it again at the other end. A doctor, nurse and two porters with a stretcher ran past shouting about an emergency. Finding the ambulance empty, they ran back to her.

'Are you the emergency?' they asked.

'I don't know,' she replied. 'There wasn't anyone else in the ambulance.'

They put her on the stretcher and ran with her into the delivery room. The last thing she'd heard was that she might have appendicitis. A couple of hours later she was handed me.

'Hallo, Mum.'

Fred had gone home from work to be told that his wife had been taken to hospital. He arrived at the hospital to be told he had a baby girl, and believed they'd muddled him up with somebody else.

'Hallo, Dad.'

I am convinced that both my parents lived the rest of their lives in a state of shock. In fact, they never told me where I came from; they just kept asking me.

So, welcome to a book with the Appendix at the beginning.

2. Going Ga Ga

Dad raced to his parents' house to tell them of my arrival, but this tale of the unexpected galloped well ahead. By the time he reached my gran's house he had been pipped at the post by the woman in the fish shop. Meanwhile, back at the hospital, Mum had decided to keep me. The doctors asked, considering her age and emotional state, whether she wanted to have me adopted. Mum said no. So I stayed with this couple I'd only just met. Despite the fact that I'd arrived seventeen years after their wedding, I was also premature. Weighing in at just over four pounds, I spent my first couple of weeks, according to my mum, in an 'incinerator'.

'What time was I born?' I'd ask in teenage years, needing the information for some astrological chart or other in a magazine.

'I don't know, just as I was watching *Coronation Street*,' she'd reply.

For various technological, chronological and biological reasons this was not possible, but I always took it to mean seven-thirty in the evening.

Mum had been prescribed Guinness stout by a doctor when she was eighteen, for anaemia, and she had never seen any reason to stop drinking one or two bottles a day. After I was born, the doctors didn't see any reason for her to stop drinking it either. So there we were, Mum and me, both with our bottles, spending our first Christmas together in hospital, visited regularly by Dad. Later, we were joined by my Uncle Joe who, for some reason, had fallen down a thirty-foot hole. After Mum and I came out of hospital my dad had to go in for an operation on his ears. Presumably because he still couldn't believe them.

I was brought home amid a flurry of excitement. A non-stop stream of visitors appeared, made up of friends, relatives and the downright curious. It is not commonly recognized that at the dawn of time the true purpose of a nine-month pregnancy was to give the expectant mother and her female relatives enough time to knit infinite matching sets of miniature bootees, bonnets and cardigans. (Since those days, what with evolution, and the coming of Mothercare and Babygap, this gestation period is somewhat redundant and remains merely as a throw-back to our savage, primeval past.) My surprise arrival had thrown this biological necessity into disarray, and my first winter wardrobe was a vast assortment of hand-me-downs from the brothers and sisters of other babies. Whether these cast-offs, given to me so early in life, were to blame for my obsessive attraction to charity shops, car-boot sales and skips is probably impossible to say, without going through hours of rebirthing and therapy.

As a baby, as far as I know, I had everything I needed: loving parents; bottles of milk; and my own huge wooden double bed from my gran's house. When my mum went back to her cleaning job at the pub, I used to go along as well, for the ride. Propped up in my pushchair, I'd stare at the red plastic bucket next to me and wonder if I was a twin. Mum would kneel on a mat and scrub the floors with a hard-bristled wooden brush, because she refused to believe that the job could be done properly standing up with a mop.

With my first teeth came my first arrowroot biscuit, which I would share with the pub dog. Or maybe the pub dog shared his biscuits with me. After I learnt to walk, I tottered around the pub, and one day, when I was about three, fell backwards into a bucket of dirty soapy water. Mum had to wrap me in a blanket, leave work early and take me home in the pushchair. On the way, just before the railway bridge, my mum met one of the many people she knew. They started chatting and, when I thought this distraction had gone on long enough, I opened up my blanket and declared, 'I haven't got any clothes on!' This soon had us speeding on our way. I liked the railway bridge, because I'd wave to the trains and people would wave back.

Back at home, I could totter up and down the back garden on the garden path, a path that Dad had concreted to make safer. I was a toddler with platinum blonde curly hair, a big smile, and a nappy. As I got older, I developed (and later lost) a taste for Guinness myself. If Mum did her dusting and didn't put it far enough out of my reach, she'd come back to an empty glass and a three-year-old with a white moustache.

My constant companion was Andy, a black-and-white panda stuffed with sawdust. Andy would occasionally take it upon himself to leap out of the pushchair, and all hell would break loose until he was safely back with me and the bucket. Sometimes he'd be brought home by people who had found him lying in a gutter somewhere and knew where he lived. Presumably as a punishment, he would be rubbed harshly with a flannel and hung on the washing line by his ears. One fateful night, I woke up to find that one of Andy's eyes had dropped out. Obviously this called for emergency action, namely a fair amount of screaming until his eye could be stuck back in. In those days babies were tough, and it didn't seem to matter if your panda or teddy had black-and-white glassy eyes on the end of long metal prongs. However, Mum decided it would be safer to take out both of these eyes and sew on buttons instead. Clearly this wasn't a job that could be left to the morning, and emergency surgery needed to be carried out there and then. Just in the nick of time as it turned out, because to this day Andy has one good shiny brown eye and unfortunately no sight at all in his dull black beady one. Eventually, when I had grown enough, I had my own hand-me-downs, which I would pass on to Andy, some of which he still wears.

3. *A True Nature's Child*

To me a nursery was not a playgroup of paddling pools and building bricks, but a vast land of greenhouses bursting with hot sweaty leaves and cucumbers.

My father, grandfather, and most of my ancestors on both sides for the last hundred years, were agricultural labourers. Old family photos show men in flat caps and corduroy trousers digging the fields, and women in long dresses packing boxes of tomatoes at trestle-tables. The sort of picturesque scenes of romantic rural England that you're liable to find gracing the walls of any Berni Inn Steak House. Although only fifteen miles from central London and now part of the outer London sprawl, the town had been a country village in my parents' childhood. My cousins and I are the first generation not to work in the nurseries, although some of them live on the housing estates where the nurseries once were. Which goes to show, that even if you don't move to a new town, sometimes a new town can move to you.

My dad worked every day including Christmas morning,

with Saturday and Sunday afternoons off. The workers included the nursery owner and his son; and my dad, who was in charge of about four other men, mainly Italians who had been prisoners of war and then stayed on. Once he was clamped against the wall by the two prongs of a pitchfork, held by a swearing Sicilian — but usually they all got on fine. Depending on the time of year, he would be 'packing', 'steaming' or 'spraying' at the nursery until all hours, which were all different processes involved in the growing of these cucumbers. Dressed in his old threadbare jumper and worn-out trousers held up with a necktie, he'd be spraying pesticides in an outfit far removed from the astronaut suit recommended for the job now. During the war he'd been moved from the nursery to work at pulling barge-loads of cordite explosive along the River Lea to the gunpowder factory. This land too now has, ill-advisedly or not, new houses built on it.

Dad finally gave up with the push-bike and bought a moped. As a kid, still tucked up in bed, I'd hear him go out the front door at about half-past six each morning. I'd hear the gate scrape on the concrete path, and then the desperate whirring of pedals as he tried to get his moped started. On a good day, the 'phut phut' would start up, the metal stand would 'clang', then the 'phut phut' would continue up the road. More often than not, the 'phut phut' would cut out again soon after the 'clang' and he'd be out there for precious minutes trying to start it up again. If it was an especially cold morning, Dad would have to run up the road with the moped to get it going. Sometimes the suspense got too much and I would get out of bed and watch from behind the curtains. I'd see him hanging on to the handlebars, running up the road first in one direction and thirty seconds later in the other, ready to jump on the moment the moped showed any signs of life.

When I was nine, my dad bought a more trusty Honda 50cc. This bike had two seats, so on Sunday afternoons he would take me out for a ride. I loved sitting on the back of the bike, especially in the days before helmets were compulsory, and I'd come back with my hair in one big tangle. My dad would often turn round to tell me proudly, 'We're doing over thirty now!' and find me lying back flat out on the seat, with arms spread out wide, and my feet hooked under the footrest. 'What the bloody hell are you doing?' he would shout. 'Sit up straight!'

I liked travelling that way. My ambition was to stand on the seat, but I drew the line at attempting that one. If we went anywhere near a steep hill, I would have to get off and walk up, and occasionally we'd both have to get off and walk up. The motor-bike rides usually ended up at the nursery – to me, a magical place. I loved wandering inside the gloriously ramshackle greenhouses, amid the jungle of hot damp musty leaves. The heat and smell would become so overpowering I'd have to run outside to take a deep breath of cool fresh air. Before we left, we'd pick a couple of small cucumbers, 'crooks' they were called (as, I suppose, were we) and take them home in the saddle-bag for tea.

Once I was working in an office as a temp and, as my boss was stacking up some paperwork to finish off at home, he asked me what my father did. I told him he worked on a nursery growing cucumbers.

'Oh my,' he declared, 'you really have come up from the bottom of the pile then, haven't you?'

'At least when he brought his work home with him, we could eat it,' I replied.

The nursery was also a menagerie. Chickens would roam freely, ignored by the feral cats running around the packing sheds. Next door was a pig farm, and in the next field was a boxing goat. Towards Christmas, the cucumbers would be replaced by huge blooms of white, red, gold and bronze chrysanthemums. In winter time, Dad would have to go back to the nursery at night to check on the heating and I always wanted to go as well. Behind the greenhouses was the boiler house, and I'd watch him go down the concrete steps and lift the lever on the huge metal door. Suddenly, there would be the roar of the furnace and, as he stood there in the glow of the fire, I used to think my dad looked like Casey Jones stoking up the train engine.

4. At First Sight

I used to will myself to have the dream where there would be six of us, me and five brothers and sisters. Sometimes it worked out that I had six brothers and sisters and I was the seventh, and the odd one out, because my powers of dream control were not that advanced. If they had been, I would have purged the continual nightmare about spiders. In reality, I found the idea of brothers and sisters a very odd one indeed.

My parents didn't really know many couples with

children the same age as me, but I had aunts; aunts who were 'not real aunts'; uncles; and cousins galore, all living fairly close. Given the logistics of buses and my mum and dad working, we saw them all as often as we could. There was only one aunt and uncle that lived far enough away that they had to stay overnight, and they didn't have any children. My uncle would sleep downstairs on the settee, and my aunt would sleep with me and I'd wake up to see her teeth grinning on the pillow next to me. Not her, just her teeth.

Our neighbour on one side was a bedridden woman in her eighties called Edie, and every night and morning, my mum would check that she was all right. The neighbours the other side, Ernie and Hilda, were the same age as my parents, and had moved in at about the same time during the 1940s. Their daughter, Shirley, was ten years older than me and used to try to teach me knitting and a few board games. Although I wasn't too hot on the craftwork, I was very proud of the Monopoly board I copied out on to a flattened-out shoe box. Ern was a staunch Labour supporter, but had joined the Conservative Club because the beer was cheaper.

My aunt also carried out similar acts of subversion. On election day, she would go to the polling station in the car the Conservative candidate provided, and then vote Labour. This gave her a thrill for two reasons: one, the Conservative car was usually posher; and two, she figured that while they were taking her to the polling station, they could not be taking a Tory voter. Dad always voted Labour, but Mum would vote Conservative because she reasoned that, being wealthier, a Conservative government would have more money to spend on the rest of us.

Books never figured highly in our house. I had a few old books with no pictures in, that I used to scribble over, and my parents had the *Old Holborn Book of Boxing* that my dad got free with his tobacco wrappers. My dad smoked roll-ups, and I used to like making them with the Rizla papers in the little metal-and-rubber machine. He only smoked four or five a day, but I used to fill up the tin for him. In retrospect I suppose this meant either that they were dried up when he smoked them, or that he smoked more than he wanted to. Shelves weren't for books, they were for ornaments, and we were never short of a china crinoline lady holding an umbrella, or a pottery figure sitting on a bench, with my mum's own embellishments. We had a large brown pottery poodle that wore an outsize pair of orange plastic spectacles that came out of a Christmas cracker, and a Babycham bambi from the pub that wore a maroon-and-white spotted bow-tie. She collected some cockle-shells on holiday, brought them home and placed them on the heads of the pottery cobbler, the old people in rocking chairs, and the elegant Regency courting couple, so they all looked like my dad in his flat cap.

As far as theories on the sociological stereotyping of gender were concerned, my parents, thanks to hand-me-downs, were way ahead of their time. I had dolls of various shapes, sizes and colours, but my favourite toys by far were my Dinky cars and my metal clockwork train set.

I'd never seen so many other kids to play with at one time as on my first day at school. When my mum came to take me home for lunch I couldn't be found. The teachers were put on alert, and I was eventually discovered in the canteen, tucking into the school dinner that I hadn't paid for. I didn't want to go home just then because I'd spotted the rice pudding, and Mum decided I might as well stay. This decision, made so early in life, sealed my fate, and I was subjected to school dinners for the next thirteen years.

School had its ups and downs, but generally I liked it. I used to take books home, and always hung around at the end of the day to get one of the left-over bottles of milk. The girls would skip with a rope made up of hundreds of elastic bands tied together, and swap diamonds that we'd dug out of our mums' brooches.

A lot of the other kids already knew each other or had older brothers and sisters at the school, but as I was a little bit reticent, and without immediate protection, I was open to being bullied. My particular little fiends were a girl called Diane who, in retrospect, resembled a very young Margaret Thatcher, and whose speciality was pinching my arm. She shared me with Gary, a little thug who in his twenties fell off a motorway bridge and broke both legs. I have got an alibi.

After I started school, my mum became the lunch-time barmaid at the pub, as well as doing the cleaning. There was a room upstairs full of junk and magazines where I used to play in the school holidays. A serving hatch faced out on to the bar, so Mum and I could check on each other. Unless they were especially busy, it would only take a couple of calls before a nice hot steak-and-kidney pie would be pushed through the hatch. If another kid was left outside with a lemonade and a packet of crisps, Charlie, the publican, might suggest they came in so I'd have a companion. Usually they were a little more adventurous than me, and would start opening up cardboard boxes to see what they could find. Once, a boy and I found this stack of old 78 records, and a wind-up gramophone. He discovered that if we put them on the turntable, spun it round really fast, then stuck a dart in the groove, we could hear the music. The whole collection must have been ruined by this experiment. A different kid and I took out all the inner workings of an old carriage clock, and left it up there with springs, cogs and pendulum all over the floor. While I don't remember anything being said to me about these incidents, some kids didn't seem to be invited again. If I was on my own up there, as long as the meat pies kept coming, I used to be happy colouring in the cartoons and drawing moustaches and glasses on the ladies in the magazines.

The first boy I fell in love with at school was Duncan, when we were both six years old. One lunch-time, as usual, he was sitting surrounded by a group of adoring girls. We all watched as he stretched out to a clump of tiny daisies and started to pick them. He made a little bouquet and looked around at the girls' excited faces, and then over to where some other girls were playing. Finally he gave the bunch to me. I was ecstatic.

'Go and give these to Anne,' he said, and I did.

After a year or so, Duncan and his family moved back to Scotland and left a class of heartbroken little girls. Of the other boys I liked, one emigrated to Australia, and another one, who didn't go away, in no uncertain terms used to tell me to.

At school, there were some girls who looked trendy by the age of seven and looked like they were heading towards the right overall shape. I was a tall but slightly podgy little girl, with bobbed mousy hair scooped to one side and held there with a bow. I wore clothes that I would, no doubt, at some point in the distant future, possibly grow into.

My overall image was not improved upon by the fact that I was becoming more and more short-sighted. Having measles had apparently affected my eyesight, although no one knew it at the time. In class, the teacher would write everything up on the board, and we'd copy it down into our exercise books. Whenever I complained that I couldn't see the board, he would move a few desks. Then if I mentioned it again he'd say, 'See if that makes it any better,' and whack me around the head.

It didn't.

The teacher in the next year had the bright idea that I might need glasses, and the whacks and headaches stopped. An appointment was made for me at the eye clinic in a road rather sadistically named Blindman's Lane. I'm sure my teacher had my best interests at heart when she suggested I walk up and down the aisles between the desks, showing off my wonderful new pink metal National Health glasses to the rest of the class.

Once I had the glasses, I had a better view of a framed photo on the wall that the headmaster was always showing us. Here, in this primary-school football team, we could just make out the picture of Cliff Richard. It made us feel a connection with the glamorous side of life. My aunt would often tell me how Cliff, and presumably an early version of the Shadows, used to rehearse at home, and his family got evicted because the neighbours complained about the noise.

'I bet they're clamouring to get tickets to hear him now,' she'd say.

I think that the sight of Cliff, travelling the known world on a double-decker in the film *Summer Holiday*, placed a seed in my mind. I wanted to travel.

5. Birthday Lavatory

I don't know what sort of parties Cliff Richard went to in the early sixties, but my birthday parties consisted of only girls, aunts, and one 'not a real aunt' who would turn up later in the evening for a glass of Harveys Bristol Cream. My mum would rush about trying to keep the kids downstairs, and the kids would rush about trying to keep the fish-paste sandwiches down in their stomachs. There was none of this modern-day one-upmanship. No parents booked the Three Tenors to sing a couple of arias in the Wendy House. No! – the highlight of my party was the trip to the toilet. Up until I was eight years old, our toilet was in a shed-like thing down the bottom of the garden, next to the old corrugated-iron air-raid shelter. Having a bath meant boiling up kettles of water and sitting in a tin bath in front of the coal fire. All the other kids at school had a boring new bathroom, so our lack of one was a novelty. My friends would come in, take off their coats, jump around for five minutes then start screaming excitedly, 'I want to go to the toilet!'

My birthday party would be on a cold, dark December afternoon, and going to the toilet entailed a complicated ritual. Mum would help them put their coats and wellingtons back on, and accompany them individually down to the bottom of the garden with a torch. Once she realized what a hit this was, she'd save some fireworks from Guy Fawkes Night, and we'd each walk down the garden path with a sparkler instead of the torch. Once at the end of the garden, each girl would gingerly lift the latch, open the wooden door and shine the light into the toilet. Egged on by the girls squealing from the back door, she'd go inside and risk the darkness, the real possibility of a spider, or an imagined encounter with a monster. If she left the door ajar to make sure my mum was outside, the girls would scream from the back door, 'Shut it! You've got to shut it!'

As soon as she'd closed the door, the other girls would scream at the tops of their voices, trying to make her run out terrified before she'd had the chance to pull up her knickers. It was a great hit every year, and if there was someone new, the old hands would jump around this bemused girl, screaming, 'She wants to go to the toilet!'

When I was eight, the council offered people in our street a grant to have a new kitchen and bathroom built. Seeing this was the way of the future, my parents and three other neighbours went ahead. This meant months of chaos at home, with bricks, cement, pipes and all the other trappings of a building site moving through our house. It was apparently easier for the builders to have one house as the access to the site, and since my mum had been the only one to make them tea, they decided on ours.

I'd liked the old kitchen, or 'scullery' as Mum called it, with its roof sloping from a height of seven foot at the house end down to about five-and-a-half foot at the back door. Here I would help Mum with the cooking, and roll out pastry on the floor to make the grey jam tarts my dad would pretend to eat, and throw away when he thought I wasn't looking.

At home our meals were breakfast, dinner and tea. The only meal known as lunch in our house was the sandwiches my dad took to work. Dinner was the school meal I had at twelve-thirty; and tea was a similar-sized meal I had at home at about five o'clock. Dad's tea would either be kept warm or cooked when he came in later. The menus in our house pretty much ran to routine. If I had been woken from a coma, I would have been able to tell what day it was from what we were having for tea that night. Monday meant a fry-up; Tuesday, sausages; Wednesday, lamb chops; Thursday, stew with dumplings (winter), steak-and-kidney pie (summer); and Friday, fish and chips. Saturday meant corned beef for dinner and haddock for tea, and Sunday dinner was roast beef, unless it was a family birthday, in which case we'd have chicken. Since there was only Mum, Dad and me, a family birthday, and therefore chicken, was a rare treat. Sunday tea-time meant a salad, with tinned-fruit cocktail and Carnation Milk for afters. Most of the food was cooked in lard and served with peas and potatoes.

This routine did have its uses. My dad came home one evening covered in blood, because he'd driven his motorbike down a hole in the road, irresponsibly left by the Gas Board. Although I don't know how old I was, I can pinpoint it as a Thursday in winter, because we were eating stew.

The scullery got demolished and deep foundations appeared in its place. The water tap was then in the middle of the muddy trench in the back garden. Our inside door to the living room (or 'kitchen' as we called it) became our front line on to a building site.

Our house was like a furniture-storage warehouse at the best of times. There was no hallway, so the front door led straight into the ten-foot square front room, which we called 'the front room'. In here was a settee, two armchairs, a display cabinet full of brass jugs and silver-plated teapots and cake stands that my mum had won for athletics at school. Under no account was this room to be used. The idea was to open the front door and walk through this room as quickly as possible, being careful not to disturb anything. On the right were the incredibly steep stairs that I once fell down three times in one day in a new pair of slippers. These led up to the two bedrooms, one on either side of the landing, each with wooden double bed, two wardrobes and a dressing-table with a mirror. My favourite wardrobe was full of toys, but this was replaced in my teens by an MFI cupboard that was permanently held together with an elastic band. The kitchen, the same size as the front room, accommodated a wooden sideboard, a dining-room table with four chairs, the television, and a settee and two armchairs. Every bit of this room had to be edged around sideways. This room had led to the scullery, with its individual food and crockery cupboards, typically back in fashion in the nineties.

For the duration of the building work, as much as possible of this downstairs furniture had to be kept in the already crowded rooms upstairs. My mum kept saying it was like the Blitz, and we got quite used to it. We hadn't long had our telly, so Mum, Dad and me would put on our night clothes, get into their big old wooden double bed and watch the small, heavy wooden telly, which was perched on the dressing-table. My mum would often be knitting a cardigan, usually mustard-coloured, at the same time.

At home, our television was mostly tuned to all the comedy shows throughout the sixties and seventies: Dick Emery, Marty Feldman, Eric Sykes and occasionally Stanley Baxter. At school, kids were divided into two groups: those that were allowed to watch *Monty Python*; and those that weren't because it was too rude. I watched it, as my mum and dad 'tutted' through the naughty bits and were baffled by the rest of it. I loved *Some Mothers Do 'Ave 'Em*, but *It's a Knockout!*, with your average Joe Blow dressed as a wobbly giant falling over and not being able to get back up, was the show that used to have me crying with laughter.

When it came to bedtime, I would get out of this bed, walk across the landing, climb over the kitchen cupboards, and get into my own big old wooden bed, carefully putting a chair up against the door in case I tried to sleepwalk. I'd done it once. I'd walked down the stairs into the kitchen, woken up staring at the clock striking midnight, and had started screaming.

Downstairs, the builders had knocked out our back window to get everything through, so our first bit of new technology were some french windows, which we could walk through into the garden. Of course we never did, because there was nowhere else the table could go apart from in front of this window.

Much later, we went through a phase in our street when the drains kept getting blocked, and we'd have to call in the council. The men would fiddle about down the man-holes and eventually pull up on the end of a stick large pairs of women's bloomers. These blockages turned out to be caused by an old woman who lived a couple of doors away, who'd confused her toilet seat with a top-loading washing-machine her son had bought her. I dread to think of the state of the washing-machine.

We always had our holidays in the second week of August, and the usual guest-house in Great Yarmouth had been booked well in advance. As soon as I learnt joined-up writing it was my job to write the confirmation letter of the dates of our holiday. Mrs Mills' guest-house had an outside toilet too, so it suited us as a real home from home. That year our holiday time was fast approaching and it didn't seem as if the extension was going to be finished before we went away. The builders told us to go and not to worry. Dad wanted his holiday; Mum thought we couldn't let Mrs Mills down; and God knows what I'd have done – so we had to go.

Great Yarmouth was a great place to go on holiday

because, come rain or shine, or even a gale off the North Sea, there was always so much to do. Every year, on holiday, we threw out our daily food routine and adopted an entertainment routine for the week. There were at least four main theatres, including one on each of the piers. The first Saturday we'd probably only be able to get tickets for the matinée show, then we'd go to the fair afterwards. Sunday we'd go to a show; Monday, a show; Tuesday, the greyhound stadium; Wednesday the circus; Thursday a show; and Friday the fair again. After the shows, we would wait around to collect autographs from stars like Des O'Connor, Dickie Henderson, Mike and Bernie Winters. Ken Dodd opened up a counter at the stage door, and let everyone into the theatre.

'How old are you?' he asked me.

'Eight,' I said.

'Come back when you're eighteen,' he laughed, 'and I'll get you into the chorus line.'

I did actually think of turning up to his show ten years later for a joke. That would have been the longest pause before a punchline.

My mum came home from work one day and gave me a piece of paper with the name 'Mick Jagger' written on it.

'Where did you get that?' I asked.

'He came into the pub,' she said. 'Wanted directions to the post office.'

I thought about it, but then glued it into my book anyway.

At the fair, I started going on the roller-coaster from about three years old, when I'd been huddled tightly between my mum and dad, and barely able to reach the safety-bar. Once, when I was about seven, we sat behind the man who worked the handbrake, and I screamed all the way round because I thought he was going to fall off his seat. I couldn't go on it again for a good few years after that.

All week my parents tried not to think of what the builders were doing back at home. The next Saturday evening, we got off the coach and turned the corner into our road.

'Well, at least the house is still here,' Mum said.

Warily, she opened the front door. The front room was all safe. We walked through to the 'kitchen'. It had been redecorated, with the white, yellow and orange wallpaper that was all the rage then, and the furniture had been put back in exactly the right place. These builders must have gone on to invent the Rubik cube. She opened the kitchen door, and we gasped. There was a brand-new bright yellow scullery, with tiles on the floor and all the familiar cupboards repainted white.

Ahead of us, through the next door, past an airing cupboard on the right, was a pink sliding door leading to a brand-new pink-walled bathroom, with a white bath, white washbasin and a white toilet. Mum pressed down the cistern handle, and the three of us stood in awe, staring into the pan as the water flushed down and swirled around into the bowl.

The small area between the new kitchen and bathroom doors had to provide my new party trick. I would take visitors into this small dark area, pretend our new toilet was upstairs and that this was the automatic lift leading to it. Once they had gone into the toilet, I would come out and shut the kitchen door. Kids would come out into the dark and would stand in this little area waiting for the lift to start. Sometimes they would wait a while, then start shouting, 'I'm stuck in the lift!' But most just opened the kitchen door and walked out singularly unimpressed. It never reached the dizzy heights of going to the outside toilet with a sparkler, but I guess even the novelty of that would have worn off in time.

6. *Christmas Budgie*

A week after my birthday, it was Christmas. Dad had to work Christmas morning to make sure the 'chrysants' were flourishing, and Mum had to clean up the Christmas Eve festivities down at the pub. I guess I still went with her when I was little. As I got older I stayed at home with my unopened presents, waiting, almost reaching the point where I wasn't even interested in what was in them any more.

We didn't have a car in our family, and the only time we went in one was when Uncle Joe collected us in his Ford Consul to take us to his Boxing Day party. At the end of the night, he'd drive us the fifteen miles home again, when his concentration had been improved by a bottle of vodka.

When I was five years old, Aunt Grace and Uncle Bob bought me a combined birthday and Christmas present of a green-and-yellow budgie in a cage. Hopefully, the cage was my birthday present and the budgie was for Christmas, because it would have been grossly irresponsible the other way round. We called him Jimmy. He lived on a stand at the top of the alcove next to the chimney breast. He would be let out most nights to fly around the living room, sadly crashing alternately into the mirror over the mantelpiece and the window. Then there would be a rush to get him back into his cage before he hurt himself. Somehow, then, it seemed so English, so homely and so kind to have a budgie.

Our cat was called 'Tibby', because he was tabby. We could have called him 'Tabby', but that would have been uncreative. He was a kitten of one of the feral cats at the nursery and could be a bit vicious. Quite often he'd lash out with his claws even if I was just staring at him or poking him when he was asleep, let alone when I was trying to get him into my doll's pram. Tibby left home when we had the building upheaval, and so really should we.

With Tibby gone, the next kitten from the nursery was black and fluffy, so he was called 'Fluffy'. How terrifying it must have been for poor Jimmy to see this replacement cat appear. Fluffy would sit on the front wall waiting for me to come home from school. He was slightly more keen on the trips in the doll's pram, and would stay in it for a good few minutes before running off, sometimes trailing his yellow nylon dress and bonnet as he went. One morning, I woke up to a commotion of shouting and swearing. I went downstairs to see Jimmy flying around the room, with Fluffy chasing him, and my dad trying to grab either one of them. Mum was standing in the doorway telling my Dad to stop swearing.

'You must have left the cage door open,' Mum accused him.

'No I didn't!' Dad shouted. 'The cat must have opened the bloody thing!'

'Well how could he get right up there?'

Eventually Mum got hold of the cat and put him outside the back door, then picked up the terrified budgie and put him back in the cage. He didn't climb back up on to his perch, but stayed sitting on the cage floor, looking shocked. When I got back from school, I rushed to look at him. He was still there in the same position, and still breathing. The next morning Jimmy was dead.

It was a sad day. Although Jimmy had never spoken, I was sure there had been an understanding between us. I wanted him to have a proper funeral and be buried in the garden. I found a dusty old half-pint bottle of my mum's industrial 4711 cologne and poured it over Jimmy's tiny body, in a kind of ritual. The funeral would be held as soon as I got back from school. I put the body back in the cage, and we left it outside on the coal bunker. That evening, when I went to bury him, the door was open and his body wasn't in the cage. I had heard about this at Sunday school. It must have been a miracle. Perhaps Jimmy was alive and had flown away!

Fluffy was off his food, retching his guts up, and very weak on his legs. As soon as my dad came home, I wanted him to take Fluffy to the vet. The usual method of taking our cats to the vet was to force them into my mum's shopping trolley and zip it up quickly before they could get out. On this occasion Fluffy didn't put up the usual fight, and I watched him disappear down the road, enveloped in tartan. My dad came back with an empty shopping trolley. Fluffy was suffering from severe liver failure, and the vet had put him to sleep. I burst into tears. I'd lost both my pets on the same day. As I sat as I often did for comfort, under the dining-room table, I spied, through my swollen red eyes, a small pool of sick, the trace of a green-and-yellow feather, and caught just the slightest whiff of eau de cologne.

My next pet was a white mouse, which I brought home from school in a Tupperware box to look after during the holidays. Although my mum could deal with spiders, she was none too keen on mice, and used to shudder every time she walked past its cage in the kitchen. The school had allowed me to have 'Tinkerbelle' only if I already had a cage for her at home. It wasn't a lie, I did have a cage. The bars were a bit wide, but Tinkerbelle looked happy running up and down the ladders, although as far as I know she never talked to herself in the mirror or sat on the swing.

One tea-time, as my mum was preparing to start on the sausages (so it must have been a Tuesday), she opened the cupboard door to find Tinkerbelle squeaking in the frying pan, trapped knee-deep in cold lard. After this, Tinkerbelle was relegated to the shed, which had replaced the toilet at the end of the garden. The next time she escaped from the bird cage, we didn't find her, and while Mum was wary for a while opening cupboards, it finally became clear that Tinkerbelle had flown the nest.

'Right, that's it,' declared Mum, 'no more pets!'

I felt sure she couldn't mean it, so a few weeks later I brought home a ginger kitten from the pet shop. Moving away from the more obvious, I called him 'Dusty'. This was the name he had answered to out of a list of possibilities. Whether his 'mew' was because he liked the name, or because he'd slipped off the chair, I couldn't be entirely certain, but Dusty he became.

Dusty lasted well into my teenage years, and his death came naturally, of old age at home, as he would have wished. The news of his death reached me one morning when my mother called up the stairs.

'Get up, Janie, the cat's dead!'

I came down straightaway, since this was different from the usual ruse to get me out of bed in the morning. It was true. There was Dusty, stiff as a board, lying like a draught excluder under the settee. Despite my previous intentions, Dusty turned out to be the only pet that actually did get buried in the garden.

7. Saturday Fish

My mum always called me 'Janie'. I didn't know why, and I don't think she did. I used to correct her at first, because I thought she'd got it wrong, then I got used to it. At primary school my best friend was called Jane, so this only added to the confusion. Her family were the local funeral directors, and she lived with them above the shop. Every third Saturday in July there would be a carnival along the section of the main road we called our home town. We'd watch it first pass her dad's shop, then run down to watch it again outside the pub. Obviously, since this was Hertfordshire and not Rio, 'carnival' meant a parade of lorry-loads of happy, smiling people from the Rotary Club, Barclays Bank and the Gas Board. These would be interspersed with the Dagenham girl pipers and beauty queens from the surrounding area showing off the regal wave they had borrowed for the occasion. A murmur could sometimes be detected among the expectant throng. 'Aw, she's come all the way from Harlow!'

Bringing up the rear, and getting the biggest cheer of the lot, would be Charlie Finch, the local rag-and-bone man. The event was the highlight of the social calendar and people would come out to crowd on the pavement and watch the procession. One year, the local newspaper decided to send out 'Mr Mercury', a mystery man in a mac who would mingle with the waiting crowds. His mission, which he'd obviously decided to accept, was to search out punters waving that week's issue, ask them a simple question, and then give them five pounds if they got it right. My friend Jane and I were thrilled, therefore, to be approached by a dodgy-looking man in a trilby, who separately took us down the side of the pub, asked us a simple question and gave us our winnings. Innocent, warm, trusting days, when a nine-year-old could wander up an alley with a stranger, come back with a fiver and nobody thought anything of it. He wrote down our names and our reaction to being two of the lucky winners. At the time I could have sworn I'd said, 'Blimey, I didn't fink I'd win nothing,' which I saw translated in the following week's paper as, 'It's wonderful. I never dreamt I'd be so lucky.'

English was always my best subject. I'd even been born it. When I first joined the local library I took out four books, read them, and took them back the same day.

'You're not meant to do this,' the woman told me, 'these have been stamped out for three weeks.'

So after that I did what you were meant to do with library books; take them out, then take them back after three weeks, unopened.

A lot of the kids round my way were sent to Sunday school. Mum and Dad both worked Sunday mornings, so I suppose that's why I went, rather than for any religious reason. It meant crayons, songs, and shepherds and their flocks made out of toilet-roll tubes, tissue paper and cotton wool. Going to Sunday school also meant going on the Sunday school outing once a year to Walton-on-the-Naze. My cousins, Sue and Gill, went to a different Sunday school, so it meant I'd go on their trip and they'd come on mine. I was known for taking with me a battered brown weekend case that my mum had packed completely full with fish-paste sandwiches.

Saturday mornings for a while meant ballroom-dancing lessons in the function room above the Falcon pub. The kids with an aptitude for the foxtrot got to be tarted up in miniature ballroom dresses and entered for the medals and championships by overly ambitious mothers. Most of us were left to plod woefully around the room, muttering 'one two three, one two three', with someone much younger and much shorter than ourselves. To this day, I can only waltz with someone whose arms are outstretched upwards, and whose feet are not quite touching the ground.

Saturday afternoons for a while meant football. Round our way, you inherited a football team, and supported it without question. Our team was Spurs. Occasionally, my dad would go up to White Hart Lane, and even more occasionally he would take me. Mainly if he went to the football, though, it would be to see a local semi-professional team at the sports ground. There would be about fifty or so other blokes, a few dogs, and a few other kids like me who would spend the time seeing how long they could hang dangling with their arms and legs wrapped around the rail.

When I got older, I used to go up to Spurs occasionally with a friend called Sue. After a Spurs versus Wolves game, we followed some people on a pitch invasion. I dug up a bit of Spurs turf which I took home and tried, unsuccessfully, to grow in a flower pot. After Sue got engaged, her boyfriend stopped her going because he didn't want her hanging around with forty thousand blokes on a Saturday afternoon. Even we knew there was no chance of a girl getting noticed at one of these places. I suppose I got my own back when I got drunk on tequila at her engagement party and threw up on the displayed canteen of cutlery and the his-'n'-hers towels.

Saturdays, for a while, meant working. My first Saturday job was in a dry-cleaners. I got the sack after about a year one Saturday in November. I know it was a November, because of the NOVEMBER CHEAP OFFER! sticker that the other girl and I had stuck on the back of the manageress.

My next Saturday job was in a department store, not far from home geographically, and not a million miles from *Are You Being Served?* in spirit. I worked in what was called Fancy Goods, selling the sort of things you don't want yourself, but which prove to be an indispensable gift item for someone else. To me, it always felt as if I was standing inside my mum's display cabinet. It was a painfully quiet corner, except for two weeks when there was a nationwide craze for a useless article consisting of small brightly coloured plastic balls waving about on black flexible rods. People went mad, pushing and shoving and fighting, and we couldn't sell enough of the things. Quite possibly, somewhere in Eastern Europe, starving Russians or Poles were having the same reaction to potatoes. Then, as quickly as the craze arrived, it dried up, and we were back to selling the occasional horse brass. I was moved up to Ladies' Separates, where I learnt how to fold cardigans.

As I got more ambitious in my Saturday jobs and clamoured for the bright lights, I went to work in Selfridges on the ladies' scarves counter. I also used to help out in the summer sales, but hardly ever arrived before the doors opened, and would have to push my way through desperate customers before I could get behind the counter to serve them.

Dad started to get the whole of Saturday off, and it became his job to go out in the morning and buy the haddock for Saturday tea, a task he took very seriously. Since this was the only shopping he did, it was important to him that he got a bargain. Jane would usually come round on Saturday afternoons and we'd go to the park, the Wimpy

Bar, or wander aimlessly round the newly built shopping centre.

'Where are you going?' my dad would ask.

'We don't know,' we'd reply and start to leave.

My dad would then rush to the fridge, thrust a lump of haddock under Jane's nose and ask, 'How much do you think that was?'

Jane would look at me for inspiration.

'One pound fifty,' I'd mouth silently.

'Er . . . one pound fifty?' she'd guess hesitantly.

'No, a pound!' Dad would say triumphantly and put it back in the fridge. Then we'd go out.

This ritual, disrupted only by my Saturday jobs, continued for years. Later on, boyfriends would be tested on this question. Sometimes my dad would turn round and look at me accusingly if he thought I'd been helping them. I'd moan, 'Stop showing people the fish!' – but I think it had become legendary by then, and people remarked on it if they weren't asked.

8. Pants and Ants

The school had a parents' open day to show off our work. My dad went to my old primary school and was told I had left some time earlier. I was fifteen years old. It's not that my parents weren't interested, it just never occurred to them to interfere with anything that happened at school.

In the top class of primary school, where you sat depended

on where you came in the exams. I usually came about sixth, so I sat next to the person who came fifth and behind the person who came fourth. The first ten or so kids got taught intently, the next fifteen got set things to do, and the last half-dozen got left to run riot. The eleven-plus exam had been scrapped, and whether you went to a good or bad school depended on an assessment of your work, the recommendation of the teacher, and an interview with the prospective headmaster. I think the first two must have been quite good, because I had a giggling fit throughout the third and still managed to get into a decent school.

The school I went to at age eleven was just turning comprehensive, but still had yearnings to remain a grammar. There was the school song, morning assembly and prayers, a strict, non-wavering uniform, house points for achievement, and we'd stand up when the teacher came into the class and chant things like, 'Good afternoon, Miss Butler.' My uniform was a value-for-money, large, dark green pinafore dress that had to be purchased from the sole supplier in the West End. I would, of course, grow into it, and I was still wearing this pinafore in the sixth form, when it had been restyled into a skirt. We trooped around all day, from lesson to lesson, our books in new leather satchels too stiff to buckle up, loaded up like pack-donkeys.

On the very first day we had PE, and had to carry all that stuff around as well. I went to the gym, we all got changed and ran around a bit to warm up. Finally the teacher clapped her hands.

'Now 1B, I want you to . . .'

'Is this 1B?' I chirped up. 'I'm in 1A.'

'Well you're in the wrong lesson, aren't you!' she shrieked.

The rest of the class sniggered. I got changed back into my school uniform and embarked on the great trek to discover the whereabouts of my Geography lesson.

The Games teacher and I never got on to the same wavelength. I wasn't really any good at Games, and on every school report she would write that I had 'no sense of urgency'. My glasses would always get smashed by any rounders, hockey or tennis ball that came within a mile of me. When we had swimming, I couldn't see where I was going, and I could only swim as far as one breath would take me. I'd only got my 25-yards certificate by pretending to do breaststroke while hopping along with one foot on the bottom of the swimming-pool.

Another major stumbling block has always been the state of my feet. In winter they are freezing cold and bright mauvey-pink, whereas in hot weather they turn the same colour and swell anywhere up to the next two shoe sizes. One winter's day I had forgotten my regulation navy blue knickers for Games. I was in my new bright pink underwear, trying to get my hockey shorts on before the Games teacher noticed. Too late.

'Oh, look at your bright pink . . .' she exclaimed. Her voice became so shrill it had gone clean out of my range and I didn't hear what she said. I looked down at my knickers.

'Yes,' I said, 'I got them for Christmas. I got a bright green pair as well.'

The rest of the girls burst out laughing.

'Let's see how funny you find a detention, shall we?' she asked and stomped off.

I looked at the others.

'What?'

'She was talking about your feet.'

In needlework, I accidentally machine-stitched the material to my school uniform. I was eventually no longer allowed into Domestic Science after I'd thrown flaming oven gloves out the window into the school playground. It wasn't on purpose, I'd just forgotten they were under the grill. I wasn't sorry to see the end of either of these lessons. I'd made apple crumble with the kind of golden breadcrumbs meant for fish fingers, and I'd always be waiting twice as long as everyone else for the dishes to cook, because I hadn't turned on the newfangled electric oven. Anything that was remotely edible would either get knocked into the aisle on the bus on the way home, or get flushed down the toilet by my dad, who had never got over my childhood jam tarts. The only recipe I'd ever had any success with was pineapple upside-down cake. Being banned from the kitchen was no great hardship for me.

My first acting experience was when I was twelve, in the school play. This was organized and directed by a science teacher with an artistic bent. It was called the *Insect Play* by the Brothers Capek, and seemed to be quite a popular play for schools, as there were loads of parts where people didn't say anything. I had one of these. I was a red ant. The audition for these non-speaking parts consisted of jumping up and down forty times, which I passed by being tall and not jumping up very high. Like the other red ants,

I was dressed in a red PVC tunic, thick red tights, red balaclava, and carried a gun made from a painted Fairy Liquid bottle taped to bits of wood. Our role was to step out threateningly from the wings and invade the black ants' colony. As we did this, the lights would go off, there would be a supposed battle, and by the time the lights came back on the victorious red ants would be lined up at the front of the stage. We'd listen to the red ant leader make his victory speech, then we would march proudly off. A *tour de force*. The end.

We didn't all enter the stage on the same level. Some would be at the front, some midway along and some at the back. I was at the back, six foot up on a platform, near the top of the scenery trees. Now, I did warn him. But the teacher insisted that I shouldn't wear my glasses, because it spoilt the overall look of the scene. 'Besides,' he reminded me, 'red ants don't wear glasses.' Red ants don't wear red plastic and tights either, but this fact seemed to have escaped his notice.

It was the opening night. The black ant marched towards my side of the stage. I stepped out, threateningly, and pointed my wooden gun. 'Let the battle commence!' ordered our leader, and the lights went out, the siren sound effects started up, and a strobe light flashed on and off. I couldn't see a thing; one minute the stage was there, the next it wasn't. The siren noise was winding down, and I could tell the battle was nearing its end. I was meant to be in line with the rest of the ants at the front of the stage by now. I couldn't still be stuck up on the platform when the lights came back on. In a blind panic, I grabbed hold of something, jumped down into the void below, and made my way to the front. The stage was suddenly bathed in bright light, a dozen black ants were lying dead, and the conquering red ants stood in their rightful place. There were a few sniggers from the audience. Well, what could you expect in this outfit? Our leader gave his dramatic final speech, and we turned to march off. The view behind us on stage was of a derelict timber yard. Two of the four wooden trees had fallen down, one of the black curtains was hanging by a corner, showing rubbish and tables and chairs piled up round the back of the stage. We stepped over the rubble as best we could, and the remaining curtains closed around it, to giggling and wild applause.

Time for the director's notes. He stormed into the changing rooms. 'Who managed to bring down the whole of the scenery?' he bellowed.

I looked round. Nobody answered.

'Well, who was it?'

I thought I'd lie low a bit longer and see how the line of questioning continued.

With a deep sigh, he gave in.

'Robert, lovely speech, very well done.'

The next night I wasn't taking any chances. Well before the first hint of 'Let the . . .' I carefully climbed down on to the stage while the lights were still full on, and was ready standing at the front before the sound effects had even started. This didn't please the teacher either, but that was it. The end of our two-night run. I wasn't in another school play. I didn't care, I didn't think showbiz had been all it was cracked up to be.

By the time of A levels I'd decided to do English and French, and shorthand and typing, so I could be an international secretary. The school had arranged that girls could go to the local college to learn the suitable secretarial skills. In practice this meant that if you went to the shorthand and typing you'd still be on the bus back when it was time to do the French or English. Or you could compromise and just make it to the A level classes by leaving typing and shorthand early. All in all, it meant that you failed the lot.

9. Chaste and Chest

I'd just turned thirteen when I came home from school, took off my underwear and thought I'd done myself a terrible injury. I screamed and my mum rushed over from the ironing-board.

'Oh, you've started,' she said. 'You'll get that now till you're about forty-five.'

I had absolutely no idea what she was talking about. My usual source of this sort of knowledge was Beverly, who'd told me about seeds being planted in the woman's tummy by the man. In Biology we were concentrating on photosynthesis, and although we'd had a lesson on human reproduction it was so technical as to be totally meaningless. I'd written about the penis swimming up to fertilize the egg, and then a migraine developing, but that was about it. I guess the trendy group of girls knew, and maybe that's what they'd been talking about when I'd joined in and pretended I'd understood the conversation. This had all been a total shock to me. I felt there had been a conspiracy and I'd been left out of something very important. The contraption of belts and towels, like a system of hoists and pulleys, didn't help me feel any better about it.

Some of the girls were already planning their weddings, in theory anyway. Even if I thought about marriage, which wasn't often, my vision was of me and my husband driving across the Sahara Desert in a Land Rover, with the two kids chucked in the back.

I got my first proper kiss on a school trip to Germany later on that year, among the vineyards above Rüdesheim. That kiss, and the fact that a pot of tea and an apple pie on a Rhine pleasure boat had cost me my whole week's pocket money, made it an especially memorable trip. I came back in love: he came back implying that I'd taken off more than just my glasses.

I thought my first boyfriend was about to be the boy from the youth club. He asked me to go to the moped shop with him, but he was just browsing.

The next boyfriend was when I was fifteen. Two weeks after we started going out, it ended rather abruptly when he ran up a tree and refused to come down. I stood in the local park, at the bottom of the tree, calling out his name. 'Barry, what are you doing?' But he only climbed higher.

I continued shouting up at him well after he was out of sight to the naked eye. 'Don't you want to go out with me any more?' I called tearfully, to the branches of a spreading oak tree. Bewildered people looked up, saw nothing, and walked by pityingly.

Suddenly, I spotted his older brother walking on the other side of the road. A change of tack was called for. I ran across the road and started ranting at him.

'And he's borrowed my transistor radio and I haven't got it back!' I added at the end of a long tirade.

When he eventually managed to get a word in, he asked me out. He went to the grammar-turning-comprehensive school that was the rival to ours, and though I never had a boyfriend at my own school, I had somehow managed to nab the heartthrob of the neighbouring one.

We'd regularly go to this youth club in a leafy suburban area among the country lanes, with detached houses and the occasional swimming-pool. My dad's boss lived there, so I used his address on my membership form. It was a club frequented mainly by hippies and 'greasers' who wore black biker studded-leather jackets heavily laden with chains, and who would then get the last bus home with the rest of us. I'd been there a few times with my friend Pam, and once we missed the last bus and got stranded. One of the greasers offered us a lift home in his side-car. We thought this was great, and walked with him to the car park, where we found a wooden tea-chest on wheels tied to the side of the motor-bike.

'What, this, you mean?' I asked.

'Yes, it's safe enough. I made it myself.'

'No kidding.'

Well, it was either that or walking five miles. We kneeled down on the cushions, thoughtfully placed on the floor of the chest, and he started up the bike. Pam and I peeped our heads over the top of the tea-chest, and screamed all the way down the hill. We continued screaming as the chest came untied at the bottom and sped us off into a clump of bushes, tipping us out on the kerb. He stopped the bike and came to check on us, or more likely on his side-car.

'I'd better not take you any further,' he said. 'I go along the dual carriageway now.'

We got up and dusted ourselves down.

'No, that's all right, we live quite near here,' we lied.

My boyfriend was very popular with almost everyone, and although we went out for three years, and I went with him to most of the local druggy pubs and clubs, I never took any drugs. Since I wouldn't wear my glasses, and spent most of the time hanging on to the walls and stumbling about, people quite likely thought I was on them anyway. He probably liked it because I couldn't see what he was up to.

Very early on in the relationship we missed the bus home from the club and got a minicab. Suddenly Tony looked out the back of the car and started shouting.

'They're behind us!'

'Who?' I asked, alarmed, and looked out the back window too.

'Get down!' he shouted, and he pushed me on to the floor of the minicab.

'Who is it?' I shouted.

The minicab-driver swerved as he strained to look into the back seat.

'What's going on?' he shouted.

'I don't know!' I shouted.

'They're behind us!' shouted Tony.

'Who?' the driver and I shouted together.

The driver pulled over to the side of the road. 'I don't want any trouble, just get out,' he ordered.

'But this is the middle of nowhere,' I said, from the car floor.

'I don't care, get out quick.'

We got out and, obviously thinking we were wanted by the police, the driver quickly drove off. At least we didn't have to pay.

'Tony! Who is behind us?'

'Its all right, nobody,' he replied. 'The headlights were frightening me.'

'What!'

'I dropped some acid. Don't leave me.'

There was an evening I spent holding one end of a tea towel while, on the other end, sat a confused hippy who thought it was the umbilical cord to his mother. Unfortunately, I had to have him adopted when it was time for me to go home. The chance to maybe 'hear colours' or 'see sounds', to me, was never temptation enough to overcome my worry that my brain might go walkabout and never come back.

Once Tony was in the local paper because a pub had been raided and he was charged with possessing drugs. My dad confronted me with the front page when I got home from school.

'He's innocent,' I said. 'The police planted the drugs on him.'

'Don't talk rot,' my dad said, 'they don't do that sort of thing.'

There were many occasions when the police could have caught Tony with drugs on him, but, for some reason, they had decided to plant them, and had not made a very good job of it. In evidence, the prosecution claimed that the drugs had been simultaneously found in both the black leather jacket and the brown suede fringed jacket he was wearing, when everyone knew he only ever wore an Afghan coat. Even my mum and dad knew that, because they would moan about the smell of it when he got caught in the rain coming round for me.

I was sixteen when I lost my virginity. It wasn't planned, not by me anyway, and I don't think it was by him. Tony's parents had gone on holiday, and had left enough food to last him the full two weeks. His brother, who had come down from the trees by now, had a gang of friends round, who were opening tins of food like there was no tomorrow. Tony, fearing that maybe there would be a tomorrow, but one without food, started to panic.

'Help me hide the food,' he said.

'Where?'

He glanced around the house. 'Under my mum and dad's bed!'

We walked into the kitchen, opened the cupboard, took out an armful of baked beans and boil-in-the-can sausages and carried them into the bedroom. We did intend to go out for another armful but, I don't know, somehow we just stayed where we were for a few hours.

10. 1939

On August Bank Holiday, 1939, my mum and dad went on a day trip to France. They didn't understand the frenzy and commotion that seemed to be going on, and even if they'd had a phrase book they would not have found the words 'imminent Nazi invasion'. The chaos, combined with the absence of Guinness, meant that my parents never went abroad again.

11. Uganda

One of our teachers was an Asian from Uganda, and he was keen to go back and visit his family. Being a Maths teacher, he was able to work out that if he took twenty school kids with him, the school would pay for him to travel free. Most parents recoiled in horror at the thought. I knew only that Uganda was in Africa, and that going there was one of my dream ambitions. My parents thought it couldn't be any worse than their day trip to France, so they agreed I could go.

Every effort was made to keep the price down to the one hundred and sixty pounds that the trip would cost for a month. We travelled on the cheapest, most hijacked airline and we slept in sleeping-bags on the floors of school and church halls. The teacher armed us with delicacies and gifts such as almonds and bottles of whisky. Plus, he had a magic letter that, for some reason, got us through a side door at customs on our arrival in Uganda.

Stepping on to a plane for the first time at Heathrow, amid a concrete jungle, and arriving at Entebbe, surrounded by a tropical one, was the most exciting thing that had ever happened to me. In our fleet of hired vehicles, we drove through a giant natural tropical open-top greenhouse to our lodgings in Kampala, where an armed policeman was posted outside.

The rule was that the girls were not to go anywhere on their own, so the boys were forced to be our gallant chaperones, even though they weren't averse to trying to sell us off. For three days we wandered around the Kampala streets, exploring dark doorways leading to shops piled up with goods in the cool, and the main square where taxi-drivers would fight over our custom, even though none of us wanted a taxi. One day we turned a corner and a mirage appeared. There, among the tin shacks and white marble banks, was a Wimpy Bar that could have been transported from any English high street. It had exactly the same menu, the same optimistic photographs, the same uniforms, and the same squeezy plastic tomatoes on the tables. So as not to be too parochial, we ordered the Wimpy International Grill.

On these bustling streets, blind, crippled and disfigured men, women and children cried out in desperation. It stabbed deep into your heart. You want to do something but, unable even to put your smallpox- typhoid- cholera-yellow-fever-vaccinated arms around them, you give some money and leave them to stumble on their way. Every so often, they would be rounded up, taken to the prison courtyard and shot.

We set off in a convoy of hired vehicles on our route around Uganda. Across the length and breadth of the country we travelled, blissfully unaware of political realities. When we stopped anywhere, a crowd would immediately gather around us, usually friendly, occasionally hostile, but always curious. Maybe it was the old Sunday school influence, but I bought big bags of sweets to hand out to children, plus some toys that I had brought from England. These were plastic ladybirds, with a sink-plunger-type sucker and a spring underneath. With a lick and a thump I would stick one to a car bonnet, and the children would gather round to have a closer look. A few moments later, the plastic ladybird would spring up into the air, scattering children as they ran off screaming. They'd stand at a safe distance, then come back and want to see it again. This second time they would still run off, but not quite so far, and would then start laughing. After we'd put water in the radiator, or whatever we'd stopped for, I'd give the toy to one of the kids and, as we drove off, the others would all gather round to watch again, managing as best they could without the benefit of a car bonnet.

My hair was long and, although caked in red dust, was still just visible as blonde. One group of children came up to me, pointed to my hair and then to their own, so I held mine out for inspection. One girl giggled, touched, then tasted my hair. Then everyone made a gentle grab, and we all stood in a frantic circle of hands and hair and screams and giggles.

At the Queen Elizabeth National Park, we stayed in bunk-beds in wooden shacks. It was after I'd seen the beetles and spiders on the floor that I shouted to my friend, Pat, 'Bagsy a top bunk!'

She agreed, because she'd seen the lizards on the ceiling. I lay awake all night staring at upside-down lizards darting around inches above my head, hoping they wouldn't drop on to my face.

We had our breakfast in a corrugated-iron hut, and as we were eating our usual fish and hot mashed bananas, someone tapped me on the shoulder through the glassless window behind me. I looked round to see an elephant's trunk swinging and hoovering its way around the edge of the window frame. Having become a little bored with bananas, I spotted here an excellent opportunity for getting rid of them. I scooped up a handful of mash and held it under the searching trunk. The whole face of the elephant now appeared in the frame as the animal cast its eyes over its benefactor. A chain formed across the table of left-over breakfasts, as mashed banana passed into my hand and rapidly vanished up the soft, thin, grey chimney.

Breakfast is finished. We are setting off for the day. We wander out of the hut, tread carefully past the elephant and towards the cars. In all my excitement, I've left something behind.

'Sir, I've left my bag in there!' I shout to the teacher.

'Well, hurry up and get it!'

I walk warily back past the elephant. 'Good boy,' I say, as if I am walking past an unknown dog. I pick up my cloth shoulder-bag and come back out. 'Hallo, Jumbo,' I say, as I walk past for the third time.

The elephant looks at me, then starts to follow slowly.

'Sir! Sir!' I shout to the teacher. 'He's following me!' Even in the heat of the jungle, we like to keep up the formalities.

'Don't panic!' shouts the teacher. 'Just keep walking slowly.'

I keep walking slowly. The elephant keeps walking slowly behind me.

'Sir! He's still following!'

'It's all right,' the teacher assures me from a distance, 'they're only dangerous if they flap their ears and start trumpeting.'

I carry on walking.

The elephant flaps his ears and starts trumpeting.

I start to scream and run towards the safety of my school friends. My school friends start to run in all directions.

'Not this way!' screams the teacher, waving his arms.

Thanks a lot.

The elephant heads towards them, but never forgets that I am the Banana Girl, and heads back towards me. I am running along screaming, with the elephant trumpeting along behind me. I wonder to myself just how likely it is that I might outrun an elephant across the African plain. I see a mud hut and run in through the open door. The elephant tries to follow and head-butts the door frame. Inside, I burst into tears. Inside, the African family burst into laughter. What started for them as a normal breakfast on a normal day has become the day a hysterical white kid ran in, followed by an elephant's head. They are howling with laughter, holding on to each other to stay upright. I am now also laughing, but crying with shock. Eventually the family shoo the elephant away with a broom.

The game-warden comes to fetch me.

'She's pregnant, so she's a bit temperamental at the moment,' he said.

After we found a baby hippo outside the hut one morning, I tried to stay awake all the time, so I wouldn't miss anything. A regular group of us would sit on the wooden veranda all night every night for a week, watching out for animals. I figured there would be plenty of time for sleep when I got back home.

Sure enough, I went upstairs to my own bed and slept for four days solid. My mum came upstairs at regular intervals. She'd leave a hot cup of tea on the bedside table, take away the cup of tea that had gone cold, and check that I was still breathing.

While he was asleep, General Amin had a dream of a 'new' Uganda, without the Asians. On our return to Britain, he had become a household name, and the plight of the Ugandan Asians a controversy.

12. Survival

A couple of boys at school had to spend a weekend on a survival course in Wales. Some of us, who didn't have to do this, thought it would be fun to go and watch them suffer. On the Friday evening, I set off in a wreck of a car with four boys from school.

We had been going for a few hours when we realized there didn't seem to be any other cars around. We thought we must have strayed from the route.

'This'll tell us,' said Wally, our driver. 'There's a round-about up here.'

We approached it with no sign of slowing down.

'Bollocks, the brakes have gone!' he cried.

Although none of the rest of us could drive, we all felt qualified to shout instructions in an emergency. Wally drove at the roundabout, slammed on the handbrake, and attempted to steer as we skidded across the road sideways. The car suddenly lurched and, out of the window, we saw the back wheel come up on the driver's side, and overtake us. It rolled through a fence and plunged down on to a railway embankment – and we seemed to be heading the same way. We crashed sidelong into the fence.

'Quick, get out!' cried Wally.

We struggled to pull ourselves up along the seat and out of the car doors furthest from the sheer drop. We looked at the now three-wheeled car, balanced at a 45-degree angle.

'We can get it fixed and carry on,' said Wally brightly.

'Like where?'

'I can just phone a garage.'

'From where?'

'There must be somewhere.'

We looked around us at the trees, the fields, the round-about and a pile of bricks. Wally and another boy set off to find a phone. The rest of us went and sat in the middle of the roundabout. No other cars appeared in the hour we were waiting for them to come back.

'Did you find the town centre?' we asked.

'This is it,' they replied, pointing to the roundabout. 'It's a New Town.'

In fact, this town was so new, it hadn't even been built yet.

'It's all just roundabouts and bricks.'

A tow truck appeared, with the name of a garage emblazoned along the side.

'Oh yeah, we found a phone.'

The mechanic got out and wandered over to the car.

'I could tow it away,' he said, 'but you'd be better off sleeping in it for tonight.'

'What, in the car?' I asked, slightly alarmed.

'There's nowhere else,' said the mechanic. 'I can come back and collect it first thing in the morning.'

He hooked the car up on to the back of the truck and towed it on to the roundabout.

'We'll prop it up on some bricks,' he said.

There were certainly enough to choose from.

We all squashed up uncomfortably in the car and tried to get some sleep. The first of four patrol cars stopped, and the police got out and knocked on the steamed-up window. Quite impressive vigilance. Perhaps there had been some major brick or roundabout thefts in the area.

Early the next morning, the mechanic reappeared, and towed away our bed to have the brakes fixed and a wheel fitted. We waited on the roundabout for its return and, late in the afternoon, continued on our way. The car sounded like an out-of-tune euphonium. We arrived in Bethesda on the Saturday night as the pubs were closing, and eventually found the hall where everyone was staying.

After breakfast on Sunday morning, Wally said we'd better start getting back, so we could drive home in the light. There were spaces for us to travel back in other cars but, out of some sense of loyalty to Wally, we refused to take them up.

'I'd better take this for the exhaust,' he said, holding up the cardboard end of a toilet roll.

We were driving along the motorway when Wally said he could smell fumes.

'The exhaust isn't working,' he said.

He knew there was some method of dealing with such a situation, but he didn't know what it was. Either you had to drive with the windows open, or you had to drive with the windows closed. We would have to try both. We tried first with the windows open.

'Can you smell fumes?' he asked.

We weren't sure if we could or not.

After a few more miles, he suggested we should try with the windows shut. Wally, the front passenger and the boy on my right each closed their window. The boy on my left made no move.

'Close your window, Dave,' called Wally.

Dave made no attempt to close the window.

'Close your window, Dave,' I repeated, in case he hadn't heard.

He didn't move. There was just enough room for me

With Mum and Dad as we wonder. Where did I come from?

In the doghouse already. With two of my cousins

Waiting for the AA

Ole Droopy Drawers

(*Above*) Christmas with a few friends

(*Left*) With Cousin Joan, and Andy before the hand-me-downs

(*Left*) A happy encounter with a monkey

(*Below*) Dancing queen – only seventeen

to turn and look at him. He was sitting bolt upright with his eyes wide open, unblinking and staring straight ahead. I waved my hand in front of his face. No reaction.

'Shit, he's dead!' I screamed, and tried to get as far away from him as I possibly could in a packed car.

The other two boys looked at him and shouted with fright. Wally, still driving, tried to look round.

'Shit, Dave!' he shouted. 'What are you doing?'

No answer or move or recognition. We all tried to move away and get out of the car.

'Wait till I stop!' shouted Wally, and he careered on to the hard shoulder.

We all jumped out, and stared at Dave staring. None of us wanted to touch him.

'Dave,' we called from afar.

We waved down a car, and the driver agreed to call an ambulance from the next emergency phone. Meanwhile, since we didn't know if they had done this or not, we pulled Dave out of the car, laid him on the ground and set about administering carefully timed thumps to his heart. We'd all seen hospital soaps on the telly, and felt reasonably qualified to deal with such an emergency. Finally, two ambulance men dragged us off.

'What happened?'

'He just went like it.'

'Has he taken anything?'

'No.'

They looked at us with suspicion.

'Follow us!' they shouted.

The ambulance turned into a blue flashing light and

disappeared into the distance. We didn't know where the ambulance was, and we didn't know where we were. We took the next motorway turn-off and asked at a garage for the nearest hospital.

'Did you have a bloke brought in, like staring?' we asked at the hospital.

'Yes,' they said, 'he's here.'

A doctor came out.

'Has he taken anything?'

'No,' we said.

'Are you sure?'

'Yes.'

'Well, he's had a catatonic fit. It's been brought on by taking something poisonous.'

'Bloody hell!'

'Could it be, like, exhaust fumes?' asked Wally casually, by way of general conversation.

'Yes, it could. Why?'

'Nothing.'

Dave wandered out. We stared at him.

'Are you all right?'

'I've got a headache.'

We took up our places in the car and continued on our way home. We wondered how the others had done on their survival course.

'Dave!'

'What?'

'Nothing.'

13. Training

John was a friend of my ex-boyfriend, Tony, and occasionally he went to the same club as me. He had long dark brown wavy hair down to his waist, and worked for his father's plastics firm as a van driver: a job that did not suit his artistic and temperamental nature, although he would try and make the best of it by doing the deliveries in the style of Marlene Dietrich. One night, as he was giving a few of us a lift home, he stopped the van, thumped the steering-wheel, and screamed, 'I'm so bored!' He paused as a thought materialized in his head. 'I want to go on an Inter-Rail!' he said determinedly.

'I'll come,' I said, and that was that.

In the mid seventies, among the teenagers I knew, Inter-Rails were all the rage. With a monthly ticket that cost fifty-six pounds you could travel all over Europe on the trains. Some people would take advantage of the bargain price and take a leisurely journey to Germany or France, saving perhaps five pounds on the normal journey fare. The aim of our trip was to go to Scandinavia and Greece, and everywhere else on the way. Not only this, but we added two further goals of finding the biggest big wheel in Europe, and visiting every tiny principality, city state or tax haven, to make sure we really got our money's worth. The winning big wheel turned out to be in Vienna, the clue of course being in the film *The Third Man*, but somehow we missed it. We'd gone to Salzburg and, concluding that

Austria was no more than a *Sound of Music* theme park, we gave the rest of it a miss.

We set off with our rucksacks, a tent and a hundred pounds. By the time the train arrived in Paris, we had been fined the equivalent of ten pounds for sitting in a first-class compartment.

By the time we left the Gare du Nord in Paris, my feet had swollen up, and John had already decided he'd had enough of travelling and wanted to go home. We discussed this rationally, in the same manner as we were to make all our decisions on this trip, by screaming at each other on a street corner. He agreed to carry on for the time being, to see how the trip progressed. Consulting our *Europe on Ten Dollars a Day* guidebook (there wasn't yet a sterling version), we looked up cheap accommodation. Situated in its own grounds, just back from the main road, we found an eyesore of a hostel, made of rust and grey prefabs, and checked in. Still, it was only for one night, we thought. How prophetic that turned out to be. The next morning, after a sleep, disturbed only by loud Swedish girls who seemed to travel round in herds, we were woken by the sound of armed police kicking in the dormitory door and yelling at us to get out. I clambered off the bunk, grabbed my belongings and made my way outside. The minute the last person was out, five bulldozers pulled off the main road and drove through the prefabs, totally flattening the hostel.

We got the train to the South of France, and John thought it was time we used the tent he'd bought especially for the trip. I was meant to have slept in a friend's tent in her garden once, when I was eight, but had sneaked into a spare bed during the night. I didn't feel any better about tents ten years later, and especially not about lugging them around. John was carrying the canvas on top of his rucksack, and I was carrying the tent poles along the bottom of mine. On a crowded bus in Nice, the poles got caught up and started to open out, hitting the heads of little old women dressed in black. I took the rucksack off as best I could, and at the next bus stop, sick of people shouting and pushing me, I hurled the tent poles off the bus. John then pushed me off the bus, and the conductor pushed him off the bus, and both of us landed under a lamp-post, amid piles of rubbish, with the tent frame almost put up around us. We lay there, among the debris, and finally agreed to pack the tent into one of those boxes so conveniently placed, and post the thing home. This cost us a small fortune, and arrived back at Dover over two months after we did.

A fifth of our money had now gone on a fine and postage, and it was only the second day. The next move had to be to try and save money and sleep on the trains. The poster advertising the Inter-Rail was a picture of an empty train carriage, with four smart but casually dressed young people, sitting around another young person playing a guitar. In reality, on night trains, we would be standing jam-packed in a corridor for, say eight hours, trying to sleep upright, next to a stinking, overflowing toilet and a drugged-up hippy. Anyone who even had a guitar, let alone started to play one, was liable to get it wrapped around their neck. The night train from the South of France to Rome was absolutely packed, because in August every Catholic in the world goes to the Vatican. As the train slowed down into a station, people would start trying to pile in through the doors, or heave their relatives in through the carriage windows. We were nowhere near a carriage ourselves, and had only managed to get as far as the door. This meant that every time the door opened, not only did we have less room, but there was also the distinct possibility that we would get pushed off the train altogether. An American girl near us refused to let an Italian man get on, until the glint of his flick-knife miraculously opened up enough room for not only himself but also his whole family. John and I temporarily moved into the wide-open space of the train toilet to eat our tin of corned beef and the bag of carrots we had bought ourselves as a special treat. When the train door opened in Rome, after five hours of standing on one leg, I found, in place of my feet, two huge beach-balls. I tried to step out of the train, over-balanced, and fell straight out on to the platform. John laid me on a luggage trolley, pulled off my plimsolls and cut my socks off with a pair of scissors.

On the Greek mainland, we decided that we could sleep on the beach for a night to save some more money. When it was dark, we got into our sleeping-bags, laid our heads on the least uncomfortable sections of the rucksacks and went to sleep. In the middle of the night, I woke up to the sound of half a dozen local teenage boys, who were wandering along the beach and shining a torch on the sleeping tourists. I slid further down into my sleeping-bag. They arrived at me, shone the torch and gave me a gentle kick. I slid still further down into quilted safety. One boy knelt down, put his arm into the sleeping-bag and started tapping me on the head.

'Piss off!' I said finally.

They'd obviously heard this phrase before.

'Ah, English girl!'

One pulled down the front of the sleeping-bag and shone the light into my face. They all crouched down around me.

'Hallo, English.'

I sat up. 'John,' I called.

He was sound asleep, and out of arm's reach to nudge.

'Where do you come from?' asked one.

'London,' I replied, anxious to make an ally in the camp.

'Do you know Sunderland?' he went on.

'I've never been there.'

'I have a pen-friend in Sunderland.'

'Have you ever been there?' I asked.

'When I was little,' he replied.

Another boy, no doubt bored with this heady talk of exotic places, tried to pull down the zip on the side of my sleeping-bag.

'John,' I called.

One of the boys shone the torch to try and get a better look at the zip, which I was now trying to hold from the inside. Suddenly he leapt up and screamed. He shone the torch and the others leapt up and screamed.

'What!' I asked.

'Dog!' shouted one.

'What?'

I tried to find my glasses under my rucksack pillow.

The boys began jumping backwards, shaking themselves and yelping in a very weird manner.

'Dead dog!' shouted the Sunderland-fixated boy.

I put on my glasses and they shone a torch on to a mound close to my sleeping-bag. Strobe-lit by the shaking torchlight, and half buried in the sand, was a decomposing Alsatian dog, covered in a writhing mass of maggots. I leapt up and started the same jumping, shaking and yelping as them.

'I'm covered in maggots!' I screamed.

John had eventually woken up. 'What's going on?'

'I'm covered in maggots!' I screamed again.

He shot out of his sleeping-bag and started to run up the beach.

'What's the matter with you?' he shouted from a safe distance.

'I'm covered in maggots!' I screamed once more.

Other people further along the beach had now woken up and were yelling at me to shut up. I dragged my rucksack and sleeping-bag up to the promenade, and continued shaking off imagined parasites. The Greek boys ran off in the opposite direction.

I don't know how good a guard dog he'd been in life, but in death he certainly came in handy.

14. Initial Success

I didn't hate all the jobs I had. In fact, I don't think I hated any of them. That was the worrying thing. Any one of the jobs I've had, I could have stayed there, and that was always, in the end, what made me leave.

I never knew what I wanted to do. I'd missed out on the personal careers chat with the headmistress as she refused to see me on the grounds that I was wearing too much mascara. A career as an air-hostess seemed the obvious choice then. I tried. Unfortunately, they didn't take girls with glasses. Even contact lenses weren't allowed, and guide dogs were positively frowned upon.

My first job after leaving school was in the Civil Service. I had five O levels, they wanted five O levels – it seemed a match made in heaven. Thoughtfully, on the application form, they asked which department of the Civil Service you would like to work in. I'd written 'Central Office of Information', because I'd read they made films, and I thought it could be a step on the road to Hollywood. Even more thoughtfully on the application form, they asked if there was a department that you did not want to work in. I'd filled this in without hesitation. 'Nothing to do with Accounts.'

I arrived at the main Civil Service building at the given time and date.

'No,' the man said, 'we don't have any record of you starting today.'

I showed him the letter.

'How strange. Well, if you've got the letter, I suppose it must be right.'

The job they found for me wasn't in the COI, but in an alternative set of initials.

'In the Accounts Department,' he added.

This was too much.

'No,' I explained, 'I wrote on my form, "Nothing to do with Accounts".'

'Well, it's only a temporary thing,' he comforted me. 'After two years or so, you can apply for a transfer.'

Of all the people I have met since, I can truthfully say these were the maddest I have ever come up against. That irritating office sign YOU DON'T HAVE TO BE MAD TO WORK HERE, BUT IT HELPS must have originated with these people. There was the man who kept a dagger down the side of his boot and wore camouflage clothes, although we could still see him; a retired major who would chase the girls up and down the corridor with a feather duster; a man who had some toes missing and who, if he got the girls alone in the lift, would say, 'Do you want to see my foot and a half?' There was a whole soap opera of people there. A couple of camp gays; a womanizing heartthrob; bored teenagers; and an old man whose hearing-aid used to produce feedback throughout the entire telephone system.

The job involved matching up invoices with payments, and these files were scattered in various offices up and down the corridor. We were all known by our grades: CA, Clerical Assistant; CO, Clerical Officer, way on up to EO, HEO, SEO and, no doubt, EIEIO. Under the Official

Secrets Act, which I had to sign, this is all classified information.

We'd sit at huge old wooden desks facing each other in groups of eight, and all meet in one office for our tea-breaks. Inspired by the woman who used to do her filing wearing white gloves, I wore a Sooty puppet to try and make this task a little less boring. Occasionally a reshuffled Minister would come round to say hallo, and there would be mass panic while kettles, some still filled with water, were hidden in filing cabinets.

After a year I decided to leave, not because I hated it, but because I could see myself staying there for years, firing paper-clips and paper planes. I decided to have another go at that secretarial course. I walked into the HEO's office and put a letter on his desk.

'I hope this isn't what I think it is,' he said.

'No, it's my resignation.'

'That's what I meant. Sit down for a minute.'

He took out the letter and read it.

'Yes, I can see the appeal of a secretarial course,' he said, 'but have you really thought of the possibilities here?'

I tried to think of some, other than that of going clinically insane.

He took me by the arm to his window with the view of the drones.

'Look at these people.'

Yes, exactly.

'Some of these people are five, maybe four years away from retiring.'

He looked at me to see if I had got the point. I think I had.

'There's going to be an awful lot of promotions at that time. The Civil Service has changed. Promotion happens very fast nowadays.'

He gave me back my letter and walked with me out of his office door, on to the main corridor.

'Have another think about it.'

Another HEO walked past us.

'Hallo, Dennis,' he called. 'Congratulations on your promotion.'

Dennis had only recently been made an HEO. He beamed, and nodded to me. He was living proof of his words.

'About bloody time, wasn't it?' his colleague continued from the end of the corridor. 'What was it, twenty, twenty-five years?'

15. *In the Driving Seat*

John was the only person I knew who could drive, and when it became clear that he didn't like me Like That I started to have driving lessons as a kind of warped irrational revenge.

My friend knew of a driving instructor, but warned me that her mum had stopped her lessons because he was too sarcastic. Mr Holt, a man in his mid forties, collected me in a red Vauxhall Viva and drove us to a quiet side-street on a nearby industrial estate. We swapped places and, for the first time ever, I sat in the driver's seat of a car.

'What do you know?' he asked.

'Nothing,' I replied.

And I meant nothing. I didn't know how to start the car, and I assumed you stopped it by just taking the keys out. He slapped his hand to his forehead in dismay.

'See those pedals on the floor,' he said, 'you work them to make the wheels go round.'

I began the first of my forty-four three-quid lessons that would take up most Saturdays for a year and a half. Since I couldn't practise in between lessons, I usually forgot most things from one week to the next. I had a morbid, irrational fear of falling off the seat, and would cling on to the wheel so tightly that every time I let go to change gear the car would veer towards the middle of the road.

'Let's skip the continental driving, shall we?' Mr Holt would say, grabbing the steering-wheel.

One day I overtook my first vehicle, a milk float. Evidently I was a little too close to it for the instructor's liking.

'I'll have a bottle of gold top and a strawberry yoghurt, thanks very much.'

On the way to my first driving test he gave me last-minute tips on how to pass. He said he hadn't actually taught me how to do an emergency stop because I did one naturally every time he asked me to start slowing down. He hadn't told me, and I didn't know, about the eye test.

'Can you read the number-plate of that car over there?' the examiner asked.

'Why, whose is it?' I replied.

'Could you just read it, it's part of the examination.'

We set off.

'Turn left at the next junction.'

The car in front indicated left, turned and I followed, straight into the driveway of the man's house.

The only way out was to reverse back out on to the main road.

The emergency stop I did do quite well, and then on to the three-point turn, or changing the direction of the vehicle using forward and reverse gears. I started at the side of the road, moved into first gear, drove across the other side of the road, reversed, turned the wheel and somehow ended up in exactly the same place as I'd started. I sighed.

'Maybe you'd like to try that again?' the examiner suggested helpfully.

I did try that again, and I did end up in exactly the same place. I sat and stared out of the windscreen. This was getting irritating. The examiner cleared his throat. I put the car in first gear, drove across the other side of the road, up on to the kerb, on to the grass verge back down the kerb and continued up the road. After about half a mile of silence, the examiner said, 'I think you can safely take the handbrake off now.'

We drove back to the test centre.

'Well,' said the examiner, 'you did very well on the Highway Code, but I'm sorry to tell you that you've failed,' and burst into laughter.

'Oh what a surprise,' I said.

Despite an escaped herd of cows wandering about in the

middle of the main road, I passed the next test, but I quite missed having the lessons.

16. Stepping Out

PLANES HAVE RIGHT OF WAY announced the sign, as we drove across the runway at Peterborough Airfield.

'I should think they would have,' I remarked to Keith, who now had his face pressed up against the windscreen, checking that a jumbo jet was not about to land on his Cortina bonnet. We headed into the Friday evening sunset, towards one of the wooden low-level buildings.

I'm scared of heights. I do not stand on the flat bit at the top of a stepladder. People have to prise my fingernails out of stone walls when I lose my nerve at the top of some landmark or other, and have to lead me back down to the ground. Why I thought I could do a parachute jump from two thousand five hundred foot, I don't know. The idea of a group of total strangers holding hands in a circle and floating down from the sky gave me a warm friendly feeling.

On a Saturday morning, eight of us started our parachuting lessons in a wooden classroom. The more we learnt about the jump, the more terrifying the prospect became. Our initial fear of the parachute not opening was slowly demoted to the least of our worries. There were, we learnt, even more likely problems that had never occurred to any of us. The parachute could get caught up in the propellers; at the back of the plane; in electricity pylons; or we could land on a roof, in a river or on the fast lane of the nearby MI motorway. The odds against this whole exercise going smoothly seemed to be shortening by the minute. Two people dropped out in the tea-break.

Assuming we reached the ground at any point, however, we had to learn how to land, which involved a lot of falling over and rolling. We knelt and rolled over; we crouched and rolled over; we stood and rolled over; we jumped off a chair and rolled over. Leaping off thirty foot of scaffolding on a piece of elastic and rolling over – now that was where I started to get a bit nervous. I climbed slowly up the ladder on to a structure that was like a gallows, and about as inviting. I stepped off the top of the ladder and immediately lay face down on the plank, unable to move.

'Stand up!' bellowed the ex-army instructor.

'I will in a minute!' I shouted back, clinging on to the plank.

I crawled my way along to the far end, where I graduated to a kneeling position. The girl coming up the ladder behind me decided to go back down and wander off the course.

'Stand up now!' called the instructor again.

'I will!' I shouted, still kneeling.

'If you can't do this, you can't do the parachute jump!' he shouted.

I pulled myself up by the pole, stood on the edge, closed my eyes, screamed and jumped. I landed on my feet.

'Do that on the jump and you're dead!' he shouted.

To practise using the emergency parachute, we were strung up and left dangling from the roof of the hangar.

'One, two, three, four, five! Look back, has it opened?'

the instructor would shout, along with alternative answers of 'Yes,' or usually 'No!' in which case we had to open up the emergency parachute strapped to our chest.

'Has it opened? No!' he shouted.

I hastily pulled the nearest straps, and threw off the chute. The whole contraption fell to the ground with a thud.

'We don't want that happening tomorrow, do we?' he remarked.

Sunday morning meant last-minute practice at rolling over. Two other people had sneaked off home in the night, which left three of us. Keith, whom I'd driven there with, and another bloke, called Jim, whom we'd not known before.

Stepping out in my white Bri-Nylon all-in-one decorator's overalls, a crash-helmet and my glasses taped to my face, I headed towards the plane with a mixture of terror and excitement. Maybe it should have been a mixture of Bacardi and Coke. We looked into the little Cessna plane, which would have been a four-seater had it, in fact, had seats at all. There was one, and I guessed that was already reserved for the pilot.

The instructor looked hard at his remaining charges.

'If you want to back out, do it now,' he said. 'The only way you're getting out of this plane is to jump. Got that?'

We all looked at each other.

'Yes.'

'Right,' he said, 'get in.'

We crouched down on the floor and, after a lot of

roger-type talk on his radio, the pilot taxied us off towards the runway. Our instructor leaned on his haunches by the door. At least he would have done.

'Isn't there a door?' I asked.

'No, I kicked it off when the last person wouldn't let go,' he said.

I tittered nervously, not totally convinced that he was joking.

The plane bumped along the road.

'You'd have right of way in this,' I said to Keith.

Keith laughed. Or was he retching? I wasn't sure.

The engine noise rose to screech level, the plane clattered and managed to take off. As we circled above the airfield, the instructor pointed out the landmarks.

'There's the motorway, you don't want that. There's the pylons and there's the river, but you'll hit the trees before you get to the river. And don't land in the farm unless you especially like pig shit.'

We flew over the target area so we could get an idea of where we were meant to be heading. It was marked with a large X. Or was it a memorial cross?

'OK, next time round, the first person jumps.'

There wasn't room in the plane for there to be much argument as to the order. Before this course, I'd learnt the little I knew about parachute jumping from watching war films, where everyone jumps out together. That was not what we would be doing.

'Go!' shouted the instructor, and he slapped Keith on the back.

Keith dropped from view.

'Next!'

I was nearer the door, so I supposed that was me. I climbed out of the plane, repeating the routine in my head. Right hand on the back of the wing, left hand on the back of the wing; right foot on the step, left foot on the step. Right foot off the step and into mid-air. Lean slightly forward. I added an idea of my own. Dig fingernails into the cold metal.

'We've gone past the target, we're going round again!' he shouted to me.

I stood poised as the Rolls-Royce Spirit of Ecstasy. The wind was blowing past, and up into my crash-helmet. This is what standing on the back of the motor-bike would have been like, I thought. I felt a certain calmness. The instructions continued in my head. Spread-eagle position and check the parachute has opened. If it doesn't open, there are twelve seconds till I hit the ground, so . . .

'Go!'

I felt the slap and thought I was going to start coughing.

I was overwhelmed by a feeling of utter panic.

Is this a spread-eagle position? I don't know, I don't even know where my arms and legs are. I can't breathe.

There was a sudden jolt. I looked up.

That is definitely a parachute. It looks so beautiful.

Tears are running down my face.

This is fantastic. I'm floating. Floating slowly down. It's so silent I can't hear anything. I can't see anything. Except the motorway. I can see that. Maybe I should start trying to steer this thing. Better pull on the ropes. No! Wrong way, it's the opposite! Pull the rope the other way. No, now I'm spinning, pull the rope! Now the lorries are getting smaller. I am nowhere near the pylons, the trees or the river. That's good, but I can't see the X either. Don't worry. Just enjoy the floating. My God, there are some treetops! And houses! I'm higher than a tall tree! That's so high, that must be a hundred foot or something, and I'm higher than a roof. A roof! And now there's some green stuff. What the hell's that? It's getting really close, what is it? Better lift my legs up.

THUD.

I looked up at the sky. I lay there for a few moments and took a deep breath. At least I didn't land on my feet. I sat up. A rabbit popped out of a burrow and ran off. I laid back down again.

A Land Rover pulled up near by on a gravel road.

'Are you all right?' someone shouted.

'Yes thanks,' I replied, and sat up.

'OK, well done. Make your own way to the packing shed now.'

They drove off. No chance of a lift then. I looked to where he'd pointed, and saw the familiar wooden sheds. They seemed to be miles away.

I looked around, I couldn't see the X, but of all the places I could have landed, this field didn't seem to have been too bad a fate. I gathered up the acres of parachute spread out behind me and, with this bundle of silk and ropes trailing, trudged to the shed. This was definitely the anti-climax.

'OK,' said the man in charge, 'I'll show you how to fold up the parachute for the next person.'

This was when a frightening thought dawned on us, that some other idiot, who didn't have the first idea of what they were doing, had actually folded *our* parachutes. We were glad we hadn't known this before we'd used them.

We made our way back to the main area.

'Well done everybody,' they said.

'You,' the instructor prodded me. 'You are lucky to be alive,' he said. 'We call that the 'ead, arse, 'eels, 'ospital position. What happened to rolling over?'

'I don't know. I didn't have time.'

'Let's all go and have a cup of tea,' he smiled.

We collected our certificates, and a report card on how we did. Written on mine were the words, 'Left plane with arms and legs waving.' Sometimes you can be just that bit too friendly for your own good.

17. *Biscuit Types*

Armed with my London Chamber of Commerce Private Secretary's Certificate I made my comeback into the world of work. Apart from the basic skills, we had been taught how to politely force an unwanted person out of your office, and how to cover for your boss when he was lying drunk under a table.

One of my many job applications was to the BBC.

'Can I see where I would be working?' I asked, at the end of the interview.

The personnel officer took me along a tiled corridor reminiscent of a Victorian swimming-pool. She knocked on a door, then opened it to reveal an elderly woman who didn't look up from her task of licking envelopes. The personnel officer quietly closed the door again, and we walked back to the interview room.

'Can I see the rest of the department?' I asked.

'That *is* it,' she replied.

'God!' I said, 'I couldn't work in there, I'd go mad.'

'I'm afraid that's all we have,' she said irritably. 'Maybe when the Director-General's job comes up we could give you a ring.'

Not knowing what the Director-General's job was, I replied, 'Yes, OK then, thank you very much.'

I rang a week or so later to ask if this job was yet a vacancy, was told that it wasn't, and that I shouldn't bother to ring again.

My first job as a secretary was for the manager of the Young Vic Theatre, which I got because, unlike the other applicants, I didn't secretly want to be an actress. Whenever I'd gone to the theatre in the West End, I would always be the last to leave so I could walk down to the front and stare up at the red velvet seats and the balconies. The Young Vic was not a theatre on such a grand scale. In fact, I wasn't allowed to type on Wednesday afternoons because the clanging and ringing of the old manual typewriter could be heard from the stage during the matinée performance. 'Romeo, Romeo, [clang clang ting] wherefore art thou, Romeo? [carriage return].' I loved this job, and would stay on into the evening to watch the plays, and sell programmes and ice creams. After five months, the theatre had to close temporarily until the next grant arrived, and my boss arranged for me to have an interview at another larger, national theatre.

As we both clutched our cups of coffee, my interviewer told me that she was the Secretary to the Board.

'Of course,' she went on, 'I'm wearing my personnel hat at the moment.'

I'd never heard this phrase about wearing hats before. I sat transfixed, looking at the top of her head. It was patently obvious that this woman was not wearing a hat of any description, and it rather worried me that she'd forgotten to put it on. I tried to see whether it had slipped down the side of her head, but there was no sign of it. Tactfully, I tried glancing around on the floor to see if it had fallen off. Maybe it was on seeing I was a little distracted that she suddenly exclaimed, 'I do have a few more people to see. Do you have any questions?'

'Yes,' I replied, 'what's the time?'

She twisted her arm to look at her watch, immediately pouring her hot cup of coffee into her lap.

She shrieked.

I shrieked.

'I'll get a cloth,' I said, and rushed out of the door and into the corridor, where I leant doubled up against the wall. I'd only ever seen that routine before on a *Morecambe and Wise* show. I made my way towards the Ladies, and grabbed a huge length of toilet paper, then went back into the room.

'It's all right,' she said briskly, 'I've cleaned it up now.'

Strangely enough I got the job.

The girl I worked with was the Secretary to the Secretary and Assistant Secretary to the Board. And I was her assistant. Therefore, my full title, should I have had occasion to use it, would have been Assistant to the Secretary to the Secretary and Assistant Secretary to the Board. It meant that my most important duty was to go out and buy the biscuits. Not just any old biscuits for common or garden use, but The Biscuits For The Board Meetings. I knew from my previous job just how much theatres were strapped for cash, so in my first week I bought a large tin of assorted biscuits from a stall at the local market.

'Don't ever get those biscuits again,' I was told. 'The Chairman was quite upset.' He also didn't like custard creams, pink wafers or jammy dodgers.

I was told to go to Fortnum to get some decent biscuits. I came back with some thick, crunchy expensive biscuits packaged in groups of six, which were inspected and deemed to be suitable. In the lunch-hour, I proudly laid them out on plates, each covered with a white paper doily, and placed them at strategic points on the monumental Board table, ready for the meeting that afternoon.

These biscuits were, unfortunately, too successful for their own good.

'You can't leave these biscuits lying around on the table

for an hour before the tea arrives – they put everybody off.'

I would have to bring them in halfway through the meeting with the tea.

Except I didn't make the tea. That came from the canteen, three floors away. If you kept phoning to ask about the trolley they would get annoyed and possibly not bring it at all, and I certainly couldn't rely on them to let me know when the trolley was about to arrive. The only alternative was to hang around in the corridor, waiting for the tea lady to pull the trolley out of the lift. Then I'd run through a set of swing doors with two plates of biscuits and calmly walk in at the same time. More than once, I'd get through the doors with only one plate intact. Then I would have to pick up the biscuits, blow off the fluff, and get them back on the plate before the tea lady opened the door, and the whole Board saw me grovelling about on the floor.

At the end of the afternoon my boss would reappear. 'Haven't you finished typing those letters? I don't know what you do while we're having those meetings.'

There was to be a special gala night at the theatre, and various methods had been worked out as to how to allot some of the tickets to the staff. I'd been unlucky in all of them. Finally, on the day, one of the accountants decided not to go, and let me have his ticket. In the late afternoon, I rushed out to the shops, and ended up spending thirty-five pounds, my whole week's wages, on a long black, grey and blue kimono-style chiffon dress.

I stood in the huge foyer gazing, as the array of guests in full evening wear made their way into the theatre. I was hoping that I looked just as sophisticated. Maybe I should get contact lenses, I thought. Men in red-and-gold medieval tunics were playing a deafening fanfare on long bugle things with flags hanging from them. I wondered how you could ever tell if they were out of tune. As I was finishing my musings, I looked to my right, and saw a man in a dinner-suit standing very upright, and staring straight ahead. Next to him was a man in a similar stance. I took a step forward, and looked at a whole line of men and women standing there. What are they doing? I thought. Opposite this line, and two people away from me, I spotted a petite lady in a glittering cream dress wearing a tiara.

She looked rather like the Queen.

I squeaked quietly, and quickly edged my way backwards, out of the line, and made a run for it into the toilets. Obviously, I realize now, I should have stayed and been formally introduced by my full title.

Maybe it's because punctuality is the politeness of kings that I find it so hard to be punctual. I can be late quite easily, and if I don't want to be late, then I have to be very early. Getting somewhere at the time I am meant to get there has always been a problem for me. I blame it on being, simultaneously, both a late and premature baby.

The school bell was within earshot of our house, which is usually where I still was when I heard it ringing.

Starting back at work again after the secretarial course meant commuting up to London. I lived seven minutes from the train station, and would usually leave six minutes before the train was due. It meant running up the wooden stairs, every morning, as the train was already in the station. Even getting this train meant I was already ten minutes late for work anyway. The same guard had worked there since I was a kid, and he would come to the top of the stairs to make sure I was on my way up – and I usually was, clinging on to the handrail in a state of near collapse.

'Come on!' he'd shout down. 'The train's in!'

'No, let it go,' I'd wheeze.

But he wouldn't.

Through all weathers, I rarely seemed able to get to the station on time. If I was there before the train the chances were that it had been cancelled. One winter morning, the ground was glazed with snow and ice. I ran up the stairs, straight out on to the platform and towards the waiting train. As I ran to the door, I hit a patch of ice and, with my arms flailing, struggled to keep my balance. I slid, fell over, and carried on sliding, straight off the platform and down the gap between the platform and the train. People sitting by the window helpfully tried to open the door, hitting me on the head as they did so. The guard and the driver came out, lifted me up from the rail, and helped me into the train.

Rather than curing my lateness, I would invent methods for dealing with it. When I got to offices, I would sometimes take my coat off at reception, or bundle it into a cupboard and collect it later, so I could wander in, maybe picking up some irrelevant files from somewhere, and look like I'd been there for hours. I have to say, in my defence, that I would take as long to leave the office as I had done to arrive there, and would stay working later, more than making up the time. One boss I had tells people that I was the inventor of flexi-time.

18. Horse Power

My dad always liked to have a bet on the horses on a Saturday. He probably did other days of the week as well, but Saturdays were the only times he'd admit to. Since I was a kid, I'd watched him pore over back pages of the *Sun* for half an hour at a time, muttering things like, 'That one came up in a Yankee last time.' We used to have the *Daily Herald*, a fine upstanding newspaper, which the *Sun* took over and replaced. When he had decided on the day's certain winners, he'd mark a cross on the page. Then he'd lean across to open his drawer in the sideboard and take out one of the betting-slips and one of his midget-sized blue pens with 'Ladbrokes' etched in gold down the side. One Saturday, after he'd eventually finished this ritual, I idly pulled the paper across the table to see what horses he'd chosen. As I looked through the race cards, four names seemed to be flashing at me. I grabbed a pen and drew a circle round each of them.

'Do these!' I said.

My dad took the paper and looked at the names. 'No, they're all five to one, eight to one, that's no good, you have to do the favourites. It's a waste of money choosing them like that,' he said.

'No, do these,' I insisted, 'the names are flashing at me.'

84

He gave me a worried look. 'What are you talking about?'

'The names are flashing.'

He stared hard at the paper, held it up to the light for a better look, then threw it back down on the table. He looked at the clock, and stood up. It was getting on for the first race.

'Here's a pound,' I said, scrambling for the money in my handbag, 'put them on for me.'

'You're just throwing your money away,' my dad said. He sat down again and wrote out the betting-slip. 'Give me another ten pence for the tax or you'll lose it off your winnings.' He picked up the paper again and looked at the page from various different angles, both with and without his glasses, and by wearing them and peering over the top. 'What do you mean they're flashing?' he muttered.

We watched the racing on the telly that afternoon. The first horse I'd chosen romped home a clear winner.

'I put on an accumulator,' my dad said, 'you don't get anything for one winner.'

That didn't matter because the next horse won as well.

'You've got a double anyway,' my dad said, surprised.

The next race wasn't televised, so he went off to get the results from the betting-shop.

'Well, that's the treble up,' he said, astonished. 'You've got about seventy quid.'

I whooped. We would only know the result of the next race by getting the late Saturday *Evening News*. Dad paced the floor of the newsagents waiting for the delivery. He returned home, clutching the paper and a family-size bar of Cadbury's Dairy Milk Chocolate. He'd started celebrating already.

'It's only won,' he said quietly.

I cheered. He looked at me strangely, as if trying to decide whether I should be canonized or burnt at the stake.

'How much?'

Dad got out a stubby blunt pencil from his drawer, and started to work out the calculations on the edge of the newspaper.

'About three hundred and fifty quid,' he said finally.

I went off to a party in a pretty good mood.

Dad left work early on Monday evening so he could go and collect my winnings from his regular, and therefore stunned, branch of Ladbrokes. He came home and counted out on to the table three hundred and fifty pounds in lovely, smelly, used ten-pound notes. I looked at him. He still had a handful of notes.

'What's that?' I asked.

'I put a pound on them as well,' he said.

The only advice I ever got from my dad about anything was, 'Always pay the tax up front.'

19. *Keep the Motor Running*

With my winnings on the horses I bought my first car, and somehow there seemed to be an evolutionary justice in this. It was a bright blue mini, sixteen years old, and, as the registration was AME, I called her Amy. She had been found for me by my friend's boyfriend, Mick, a second-hand car dealer in Romford. The price of one hundred pounds included: a couple of gallons of petrol he'd siphoned from a car parked near by; a 24-hour call-out service; and a fifty-pound refund when the car was finally scrapped a year and a half later. I couldn't assume he was as generous to all his customers.

For the first time I was able to take my mum and dad out in a car. My mum would always sit in the back, even if she was the only passenger, because she thought it was safer. Our first family trip out was to the local automatic car-wash, since we'd never been in one. I was careful to ask detailed instructions in the garage, as our whole household could have been wiped out by just one silly mistake. I drove up to the metal bar on the ground, wound down the window, pressed the red button, and hastily wound the window back up again. We sat there, and hoped for the best. The machine burst into life, and a forest of fluorescent green spinning brushes thundered towards us, thumping down on the car bonnet, climbing up the windscreen, and clambering on to the car roof.

'Oh my God!' said Mum. She moved to the middle of the back seat as white foam poured in through every possible crevice of the car, and searched in her handbag for a hanky. 'Wipe your face with this,' she said to my dad in the lull, as he sat there with bubbles dripping off his hair.

The brushes started up again behind her.

'They're coming back!' she called.

It looked as if we were rolling backwards. I grabbed the handbrake and held on tight as first cold water and then hot wax cascaded into the car. An eerie silence followed. Hurricane Nylon seemed to have come to a rest.

'Is that it?' asked my mum.

'I don't know.'

We had ridden out the storm, but we weren't sure about when to drive out of the car-wash. I was surprised to find the car was still in the same place as when we started, and I let go of the handbrake. The impatient driver of the car behind started to bib his horn and, as I cautiously drove out, my mum and I started laughing.

'I don't know what's so bloody funny,' said my dad.

It was a very cold winter that year, with snow and icy roads and freezing temperatures, and I didn't use the car for a while. By the time I next needed to drive, Amy had become a mountainous snowball in the street. I brought out kettles of hot water and poured them over the summit until I could see the roof of the car. I scraped the ice off the windscreen and all the windows, then, almost sick with frostbite, went back inside for a coffee and to warm myself by the fire. I dragged most of the snow off the bonnet, had a last warm by the fire, then tried to set off. The key wouldn't turn in the lock, and the passenger side wouldn't unlock either. I poured more water over the roof, hoping it would somehow thaw out the locks. It streamed down over to the bonnet, on to the radiator grille, down over the number-plate. This wasn't my car.

★

In such a bitter winter, it was unfortunate that Amy did not have a heater. In fact, there was a continuous line of icicles on the inside, along the top of the windscreen. I'd caught flu driving around in the car, so Mick came over to put in a heater, and caught flu doing that. The first day I drove with the heater on, black smoke started billowing out of it, and I had to leap out of the car and pull out the wiring. Amy finally gave out halfway up a hill in Kent, when she refused to go into any gear. Balanced on her unreliable handbrake, we waited together sadly until the AA arrived and towed her away.

Mick kept looking out for another car for me, and came up with a dark green Morris Minor Traveller for seventy-five pounds. Compared to the mini, it was like driving a tank, so I called him Tank. Rather a harsh name for a gentle motor, which had moss and mushrooms growing along the wood inside, and a free spirit with no locks. After a year I thought maybe I'd pushed my luck – so I had locks fitted on all the doors. A week later Tank was stolen.

I could have got the next car from Mick but, since my friend was avoiding him by now, that wouldn't have been very tactful. I bought another Traveller from an advert in the newspaper. I knew this car was a pile of rubbish from the moment I saw it, and I knew that the woman was lying when she protested that the engine was good and that she'd just driven it up from Bournemouth. But John, who had come with me to give me the benefit of his advice, was in a rush to buy a pair of jeans. To cut a long story short I bought this car, which on later inspection proved to have a body of filler and fibreglass, and the engine of a lawnmower.

One afternoon, having driven all the way from Brighton to London on the motorway, I stopped at a set of traffic-lights. Suddenly there was a jolt. All I could see was darkness.

'My God! I've gone blind!'

As my eyes adjusted I could tell that, for some strange reason, I was staring straight into the glove compartment. Traffic behind me started hooting and I guessed the lights had turned green. I scrambled up out of the seat, climbed out into the traffic and ran on to the pavement.

'What the bloody hell are you doing?' shouted the lorry driver behind me.

'The car's collapsed,' I said. 'It might blow up.'

He climbed down from his lorry and opened my car door. 'Your seat's fallen through the floor,' he said.

He helped me push the car to the side of the road, and I stood on the pavement with all my suitcases, until the AA arrived and towed that piece of junk away.

20. In Soviet Shoes

Debi and I regularly used to go to clubs in the West End. She had a mini so, with our own transport, we'd whiz all over the place. She was an exciting friend, and our nights out together were always fun, even if we did something simple, like have breakfast in an all-night café on Fleet Street. One Saturday night, we were in a small club in Soho, trying to get on to a crowded dance floor, which was taken up mainly by a fat man in a gold Lurex suit, waving his arms about. We gave up temporarily, and went to get a drink from the bar. As we both tried to perch on the same high bar stool, we read a notice on the wall. TAROT READINGS. LET OMAR TELL YOU YOUR FUTURE. ASK AT RECEPTION.

Against my advice, Debi decided to have her tarot read, so, as instructed, we spoke to the girl at reception.

'He's on the dance floor,' she said. 'You can't miss him – he's the fat bloke . . .'

'. . . in the gold Lurex suit,' Debi and I continued.

Despite learning this new fact, Debi still wanted her tarot read. We returned to the dance floor and got as close as we could get to Omar without being struck by his flailing arms. We mimed dealing a pack of cards at him, and he beckoned us to a table at the back of the club.

As he dealt out the cards for Debi, he suddenly turned to me. 'You're Sagittarian, aren't you?'

'Yes,' I said.

'And you think I'm a fraud, don't you?'

I laughed. 'Well, not quite so much now, I suppose.'

'I'll do yours in a minute,' he told me. 'For free.'

He continued reading Debi's cards. Within the year she would be happily settled down. We laughed – we couldn't see that happening.

He started to read mine.

'You're very soon going to a place you've never been to before, an unusual place, with a group of people.'

On Monday I would be off to the USSR with twenty other secretaries and staff from the trade union where I now worked. I'd left the theatre, as it was no place to work if you actually had to earn a living. I now had a shorter title but a higher-paid job as a private secretary to a national official at the TGWU. The 'winter of discontent' in 1979 was not the best time to admit to people that you worked for a trade union. Even we, occasionally, had to get out the manual typewriters and candles and type in the dark. With my limited inside knowledge of strikes, however, I could warn my mum when to stock up on sugar, although I could never tell her how to stock up on electricity.

Omar continued. 'I can see a romance that will come out of it.'

Of the five men on this forthcoming trip, two were old and married, two were young and married, and one was young and gay.

'Well, you're half right,' I told him.

There were to be a few more presidents yet before we'd get to glasnost. In Leningrad, formerly and subsequently St Petersburg, and in Moscow, far above the wide avenues, twenty-foot-high posters of Brezhnev, Marx and Lenin imposed themselves on pedestrians and the occasional passing bus, taxi, black limo or tank. We were the official guests of the transport workers. Delegations of union or government officials had visited before, but this was the first time they'd been faced with a group of mainly office girls, and they seemed very pleased to see us. We would visit bus and lorry depots and from nine in the morning they would start plying us with various flavoured vodkas, which we would have to down in one. I swigged down a vodka spiced with red pepper, and thought my throat had burst into flames.

They arranged for us to go to the Bolshoi – the first time

I had ever been to a ballet, and not a bad one to start with – and they presented us with embroidered shawls, perfume and balalaikas. We had brought items from the West – such as chewing-gum, tights and toilet rolls – none of which, unfortunately, seemed appropriate as a return gift. We had been told that kids in the streets would spot the few Westerners and run up to ask for chewing-gum. For a packet of Wrigley's you could choose one of their Soviet badges, maybe two for a Juicy Fruit. The tights were to be a gift for the fierce-looking woman who sat and watched on the hotel landings, and the toilet rolls were for ourselves.

Our Intourist guide, Eva, took us to museums, a term that included churches and cathedrals, and showed us the Soviet memorials that couples apparently like to visit on their wedding day. Some museums were more fascinating than others, and for some people none of them were fascinating at all. There were murmurings of mutiny among the group.

'Can't we go shopping instead?' Peggy finally asked.

Eva looked perplexed.

'I'n't there some kind of Oxford Street?' Peggy continued.

'Don't you know *anything* about the Soviet Union?' shrieked Jennifer, and a touch of class war broke out.

Eva reluctantly suggested that we could go off in groups for an hour or so, as long as we were sure we could find our way back to the hotel. Some decided to go back there straight away. I loved the challenge of getting totally lost in a city where I couldn't speak or even read a single word of the language. Two of the young men and myself had slipped out one evening when we were meant to be watching the Moscow State Circus, and had deliberately got ourselves lost on the chandeliered underground system, just for the hell of trying to find our way back again before the end of the show. I thought wandering off on my own was the next logical step.

The streets bustled with people wrapped up warm in the frosty April sunshine, and dwarfed by the heavy grandeur of the surrounding buildings. I walked into a magnificent old department store and joined about twenty people pushing and shoving to get to the counter, and holding out their money like in a crowded pub on a Saturday night. Behind the counter was an assistant, and behind her, spaced out along shelves, I could now see two pairs of men's brown shoes, a vase and a couple of transistor radios. A man next to me grabbed my arm and began using me to steady himself as he hopped about on one leg, trying to get his right foot into a new shoe. Eventually, after we had danced around a bit, he managed to get it on. He looked up at me and nodded. Thrusting that shoe under his arm, he hopped about trying on the left one, as we struggled together against the tide of bodies. That seemed to fit as well. He let go of my arm, said something triumphant, which I didn't understand but got the gist of, and gave the assistant back the shoes. She put them on one side and gave him a ticket. He elbowed his way back out of the crowd, and I did the same, slightly less aggressively, so I could see where he was going. He leant against a pillar to put his old shoes back on, then headed for a gilded cage in the middle of the shop, where he handed over his money and got his ticket stamped.

He pushed his way back through the crowd to the counter, gave the receipt to the assistant, and she handed over his new shoes.

In Moscow, while most of us shared small dark twin rooms at the back of the hotel, the two young married men had been given a suite at the front, packed with antiques, with double doors that opened out on to a balcony overlooking Red Square.

'Call this equality!' we half joked.

'Well, it doesn't matter,' they said. 'You can all come in here anyway and watch the procession.'

Soldiers lined the route of the May Day Parade. From our vantage point on the balcony we watched a red sea of banners and flags approaching along the main street, to the accompanying roar of military bands. We couldn't believe how close we were to the action – and we were right not to believe it. Suddenly the hotel-room door opened, and two plain-clothed security men rushed in. The first one asked us to move back into the room. We started to moan and argue, as we are used to doing in our culture. The man repeated his request rather more loudly, which made us move significantly more quickly. He pulled the doors shut and drew the curtains, while the second man turned on the television, showing the May Day Parade in glorious black and white. They both stood guarding the doors, in case we tried to storm the balcony.

'Do you want to go down into the street?' I whispered to Billy, the young unmarried man, and a keen photographer. As the diverting discovery of a drinks cabinet was being made, we took our chance and our cameras and slipped quietly out of the room. We walked out of the hotel's main doors, into an area outside that had been roped off for tourists. Women in smart white uniforms stood behind trestle-tables decked with red carnations. They poured tea from big ornately decorated pots into delicate china cups, replacing the pots on to huge silver urns full of boiling water. The parade continued past.

'Let's get in the middle of it,' Billy said.

We ducked under the rope and into the main throng of flags, slogans, bands, banners and balloons, as the procession of people made its way into Red Square, ready to listen to the speeches with dutiful expression.

We stayed to the very end. We watched the crowds disperse, and uniformed men on horseback gallop across the cobbled square, anxious to get the area back to normal as quickly as possible. Old women, with brooms made from twigs, began sweeping up non-existent litter. We watched some lorries arrive and, as they drove past us, they suddenly sprayed the square, and us, with cold water.

Debi was happily settled down within the year. The young unmarried man turned out not to be gay.

21. Bedsit Land

Billy drove me to the driveway of the Victorian detached house where I was going to live. I opened the front door and walked into the spacious circular hallway, with its black-and-white tiled floor and a sweeping staircase, leading up to the dozens of rooms upstairs.

'It's lovely, isn't it?' I said.

'Yes, it's nice.'

'My room's down here,' I said.

I led him through a door, and turned on the light before taking him down the steps to the basement and into one of the twenty-six bedsits in the house.

'Da-da!' I announced.

I gave him a tour of my first home. From the bed, past the dividing shelves, into the kitchen with a sink and Baby Belling one-ring cooker, and over to the window. It wasn't a long journey. I looked up from the window at an angle, and could see the roots of the trees.

'We'd better get your stuff in from the mini,' Billy suggested. 'That's if it all fits in.'

Each time I walked into that hallway I could imagine I lived in the whole house – and since it cost me a third of my wages each week I certainly felt I was paying for the whole house. It was in a leafy part of North London called Swiss Cottage, and I thought the alpine air might be good for me. The property company kept reminding me that I was paying for the area. Obviously not the area of the room. So what if a speeding electricity meter made it cheaper to go out than stay in? It was my very own bedsit. When the six-month contract ran out the company decided to put the rent up some more. I knew I couldn't afford that, so I had to look for somewhere else.

'We'd like to keep your curtains,' the estate agent said. 'We'll pay you for them.'

What, the pair of curtains I'd got from a jumble sale for ten pence?

'I had them made at John Lewis,' I said. 'They were about . . .' I named a figure that was just under two weeks' rent.

'Yes, that's fine,' he said.

Trudging around agencies trying to find another bedsit in the area gave me the chance to meet landladies from a previous century.

'I don't mind you playing music, as long as it's classical music,' said one, as the smell of damp and boiled greens wafted past. 'And I like all my tenants to be in by eleven at night.'

'I sometimes don't go out till eleven at night,' I said.

'I don't think you're the sort of person we would want here,' she told me.

I eventually moved into a large semi-detached house divided into bedsits. In fact, not only the house, but the rooms too were divided into bedsits. I was separated from the tenant next door by a wall probably made of egg boxes and held up by sticky-back plastic and wallpaper. This divider continued to the window, of which I had half, and the small balcony outside, which was divided in half by a piece of string. Although I did hear my close neighbour most nights, unbuttoning his cardigan, I only met him once, when we both opened our doors at the same time, a feat in itself. I had wondered what he looked like, and I should have guessed. A small thin twitchy man in his fifties looked at me nervously, then said, 'Do you know Birmingham Council Offices water rates are five hundred pounds a week?'

'That's quite a lot, isn't it?' I said.

'Oh yes!' he exclaimed. 'And that doesn't even include sewerage!' and disappeared back into his half room.

I tried to look in, but the door didn't open wide enough for me to see anything. Maybe it was like mine, and he too could only open the door until it hit the wardrobe, and then walk over the bed. When I inspected my mattress to find out why it was quite so uncomfortable, I discovered that far from being interior sprung it was interior stuffed, with old newspapers, and some Japanese comics that made conveniently close bed-time reading.

The landlady was a well-to-do old lady who liked to mother her tenants. These were about a dozen – mainly foreign students, except for my neighbour, of course, who it turned out had lived there for over thirty years. On Saturday afternoons she prepared tea in her lounge for any passing members of her brood, with scones, dry biscuits, and Stilton cheese so mature it should have had a congratulatory telegram from the Queen. However quietly you crept past the door, there she was, ready for a chat, and however many times I explained and demonstrated to her that my glasses had trendy mauve-tinted lenses, she would still sympathetically ask me, 'Have you been crying? You're homesick, aren't you, dear?'

22. Dad

It was a Wednesday morning in May 1980. Mum phoned me at work. She never phoned me at work. She never even liked using the phone, so I knew it had to be something important. My dad had been taken into hospital. It was nothing to worry about. He just couldn't breathe properly. She was going back there now. I phoned the hospital.

'I think it's best you come over straight away.'

We sat next to Dad's bed. He was wearing an oxygen mask.

The ward sister came along and asked us into her office.

'I'm sorry, but we don't give him very long,' she said bluntly.

Mum and I looked at each other.

'About a fortnight,' she continued.

'What do you mean?' I asked.

Obviously thinking she'd been plain enough, she replied, 'Well, obviously it's been coming – you know he's got cancer.'

'No,' I said.

'Well, hasn't anybody told you?' she asked, annoyed. She sighed and started flipping through the file, turning over letters. This one-minute task was now beginning to drag on for her. 'He's been an out-patient at two different hospitals for over a year!' she said in exasperation.

'That was just because of his cough,' my mum said.

'He's got lung cancer!' the sister almost yelled in disbelief.

I wasn't sure whether I was going to cry or punch this woman in the mouth. I knew which one I wanted to do.

'Does he know?' I asked.

'Yes.'

Mum and I looked at each other again. We weren't convinced that he did.

'Maybe you'd like to see him again now?' she suggested.

We walked back to his bedside.

He took off the mask. 'What did she want you for?' he asked.

'Just to fill in a few forms,' I lied.

He nodded contentedly.

On Friday my mum rang me at work.

'They're letting your dad come home. We've got to go and collect him.'

I went to my mum's, and Ron, now the landlord of the pub where my mum still worked, drove us over to the hospital. My dad was all dressed, ready to go, sitting on a chair next to his bed.

'How can he come home?' I asked a nurse. 'He was on oxygen last night.'

The nurse opened a plastic carrier bag, 'That's why we're giving you these,' she said proudly.

I looked in. 'What, an asthma inhaler?' I exclaimed.

'There are some pills in there as well. It's all written on the boxes, what to do with them. Besides, he asked to go home,' she added defensively.

'Surely he should be taken in an ambulance?' I said.

'Not an emergency, I'm afraid.'

'Well at least we can find a bloody wheelchair some-where, can't we?'

'I'll be all right,' my dad said.

'No, you sit there, Fred,' said Ron. 'You can't walk all that way.'

The nurse made a phone call, and eventually a wheelchair was found on another ward. We took him out to the car.

'I never said anything about coming home,' Dad said to me.

It was clear when we got home that he would never get up the stairs, and Ron brought round a single bed to set up for him in the back room. Mum and I spent the night in the armchairs either side of him. A terrifying night. Exhausted, and very very frightened, we called the doctor in the morning. My aunts arrived, along with Ernie from next door, and a couple of the workers from the nursery.

The doctor looked contemptuously through the assortment of tablets and inhalers we'd been given. 'This is ridiculous,' he said, and threw them into the dustbin. 'All he needs is this.' He gave us a tablet to give Dad last thing that night.

Mum and I again spent the night in the armchairs.

Breath.
   Breath.
   Breath.
   You will the next breath. Sometimes there isn't one.

Somehow it was beyond crying. We phoned the doctor and my school friend, Jane, who was now a funeral director. My mum coped, as she always did, by finding some work to take her mind off things. She walked into the kitchen and took the familiar frying pan from out of the cupboard under the sink and heated up the lard. We quietly tucked into our fried eggs, sausages, bacon and tomatoes as dad lay in bed alongside and watched over us.

Bye, Dad.

23. *Ballroom Blitz*

Mum did not want to spend the next Christmas at home, so the two of us spent four days in a hotel in Central London.

We looked at our Yuletide brochure to find the first event. 'The manager and his staff welcome their guests to a Christmas Eve glass of mulled wine in the Montague Lounge.' Mum didn't like wine, mulled or otherwise, so the manager and his staff reluctantly found a Guinness for her from the bar. Gradually, the hotel guests made their way to item two on the seasonal agenda 'Dancing in the Ballroom', which we discovered was down a narrow flight of stairs in the basement. Considering that most of the guests were pensioners, all except myself in fact, and that some had walking frames, this was slightly unfortunate. Metal chairs were passed over white permed heads as people carefully edged their way down the stairs. Far from the expected Louis XIV glittering ballroom, we found ourselves in a room the size of the average carpet sample. At the end of the room, and therefore very close, was a stage surrounded by red velvet curtains and set up with microphone, drums and electric organ. Metal chairs lined the three remaining walls, and rapidly the floor was disappearing, as this row became the back row, with two, three or four rows in front. The least able were now being carried into the ballroom, which no doubt brought back memories of the Blitz, or even of the *Titanic*. Eventually, with Christmas rapidly approaching, a man in a dinner-jacket took the stage.

'Is that everyone now?' he asked, struggling to be heard over the noise of metal scraping on veneered dance floor. One hundred and fifty of us were now jammed into this crate of a ballroom. Some people who had been in the first batch down now needed to make their way back up the stairs to the toilet. The MC looked at this chaos in dismay.

'Do we really *need* all these chairs?' he asked.

'Yes!'

'OK then,' he quickly conceded, 'we'd better get on, so will you please welcome the Roy Thoms Trio.'

Those that had room started clapping as three men in dinner-jackets appeared from a door opposite the stage. Two were in their fifties, and, sitting on their linked arms, hanging on to their shoulders, was a frail man in his early eighties. They carried him to the drums and placed him on the seat.

'Good evening, ladies and gentlemen. We are the Roy Thoms Trio. Take your partners please, as we start off this evening with a foxtrot.'

'There's no room,' a frail voice called out, 'there's no room to dance.'

'There aren't even any decorations,' called somebody else, and there weren't. Two couples stood up and, by doing so, filled the whole of the dance floor. They swayed gingerly in time to the music, avoiding outstretched support tights. For about an hour, people sat through the foxtrots, the waltzes and the Gay Gordons, while a waitress came round and handed out free raffle tickets.

The MC came back on stage. 'While the band are having a rest, we'll hold the raffle. Now, let's have you on your feet. Come on everybody, stand up. Come on, get up.'

Amid puffs and groans and the now-familiar sound of metal scraping wood, he continued. 'Right now, when I call out your number you can sit down.' He put his hand into the biscuit tin, pulled out a ticket, and unfolded it. 'The first number – cighty-seven.'

'Yes, I've got it!' called a shaky voice.

'OK, you can sit down then.'

'Have I won?' she asked.

'No, love, you can sit down. The last person standing wins the cake.'

It was then that the sharper of us realized, with certainty, that he intended to call out all one hundred and forty-nine losing tickets.

'Thirty-two.'

'Yes!'

'Sit down.'

The final roll-call on Judgement Day couldn't take any longer.

'I want to sit down,' pleaded a voice.

'You can't till your number's called,' said the MC.

'But I've got arthritis,' she continued.

'Seventy-two.'

I sat down.

'Is that your number?' my mum asked.

'No, it isn't.'

'One two seven, sit down.'

'I'm sitting down and so's she,' called a woman as she pulled her friend down into the seat beside her.

'Yes!' came the cries, 'I want to sit down!'

'Not long now,' called the MC. 'Number four.'

'Let the next person have the bloody cake!' called a male voice.

'I don't want it, I've got diabetes!' a voice piped up.

'All right,' called the MC, perturbed by this increasing tide of rebellion, 'whoever wants the cake can have a bit each. Here's the band.'

The band, their break cut short, relatively rushed back on stage.

On Christmas afternoon, a television quiz was to be held in the Mountbatten Room at two-thirty. We opened the double doors to find rows of the familiar metal chairs, and a dozen people sitting with pencil and paper poised, listening intently to a cassette player perched on one of the chairs.

'Question twelve. What is this TV theme?' its tinny voice asked.

'Oh, *Coronation Street*,' an excited voice whispered loudly, and they all wrote it down. We closed the doors.

'I'd rather watch the telly,' Mum said. We went back up to our room. The TV was on a small trolley placed, rather interestingly, under the wash-basin. I grabbed hold of the trolley and, as I pulled it out from under the pipes, both leads came out of the back of the telly. To the sound of my mum tutting I went down to reception to ask for another one.

I was almost beaten back to the room by a distinguished-looking man in his late fifties, smartly dressed in a dark green hotel uniform. Under his arm was a television. 'Just in time, I hope,' he said, rushing in, slightly out of breath.

Mum and I sat on our beds to give him as much room as possible. Crawling under the wash-basin, he prised the old television out and placed it on the floor. He unwrapped the cable around the new telly, puffing and struggling to get it on to the trolley. He turned on the switch, and it glimmered into action. 'That seems to be all right,' he said.

He lifted the broken television off the ground, started to stand up, then stopped dead. Mum and I looked at him, then at each other. Slipped disc, we thought.

'Are you all right?' asked Mum.

He didn't reply. Alarmed, we got up off our beds.

'Send her victorious, happy and glorious,' sang the television. 'Long to reign over us, God save the Queen.'

The national anthem stopped. He stood up and clicked his heels. He turned to see us standing by our beds in silence, and smiled, happy with the world.

'Sorry you missed the beginning, but you'll get the whole of the Queen's Speech now,' he said contentedly.

Broken television under his arm and head held high, he marched proudly and patriotically out of the room.

24. Writing on the Wall

The more people I met who had degrees, the more I thought about going to university. I did like my job at the union, but the thought that I could stay there until I was put out to graze filled me with horror. I'd been doing A levels at evening classes, and so, despite my mum's misgivings that I'd be too old to wear the school uniform, I applied to university. After four interviews and four rejections, I told the last one I was too busy to come for an interview, and got accepted.

I went off to Sussex University to do International Relations, leaving my job and my bedsit. I thought that maybe after the course I could be a foreign correspondent, or work on documentaries, or at least be able to say, 'Back to the studio, this is me, *News at Ten*, Bangalore.'

Leaving London also meant leaving a boyfriend, who I'd only just met (when we'd both realized that however interesting Mao's Long March may be, we were both going to History evening classes mainly to see each other). On Friday nights, after I'd moved to Sussex, he would cycle the sixty miles from London, usually through pouring rain and being narrowly missed by several Range Rovers, and would arrive exhausted, in a foul mood, and fit for nothing except a row. Gradually, each week, he would stay longer and longer with me in Brighton, until eventually he also ended up doing a three-year university course.

In an effort to join things, I went along to the Drama Society. They were already in rehearsal for a play, and a woman was standing on stage screeching, 'I am not a sex object!'

I asked if there was anyone else in it. There were parts for a couple more people.

'We'll be taking this play to Edinburgh,' the director told me.

'What's the point of that?' I asked. 'We all live in Brighton.'

Never having heard of the Edinburgh Festival was my ticket out of this group. It also meant I never got to appear in a version of *Cabaret* where the nightclub dancers wore calf-length baggy dresses and Doc Marten boots.

Although I was not in this musical, Berlin still featured quite heavily in my life then. By the end of summer 1982 I had already spent three months trying to write a final dissertation on the Cold War and the Berlin Wall. Right, I might as well go and see it, I thought, and set off on the 26-hour bus journey to West Berlin.

At breakfast in the hostel I met an English student called Peter, who spoke fluent German. He was going across to the East that day, and I asked if I could go with him, since I didn't fancy going on my own in case they didn't let me back into the West.

We rode on the U-Bahn underground train to the border, through blocked-off East Berlin stations where the train didn't stop, and armed guards patrolled the platforms in the half-light. At Friedrichstrasse Station we had to get off and walk through a starkly lit corridor of guards sitting behind windows, scrutinizing our faces and our passports.

We wandered around East Berlin, and started looking for the Berlin Wall. We couldn't see it, and it felt a bit ghoulish to ask.

'Where is that wall? You know, the one that keeps you

prisoner here in the Soviet bloc? We're tourists, you know, just here for the day.'

After a beer and a sausage at an outdoor café, we began wandering again, and still couldn't find it.

In the end, Peter had to ask. The woman pointed down a road, which we went down, and there, indeed, was a ten-foot high whitewashed wall. We meant the Berlin Wall. What was this? It looked like some sort of car park. It was impossible to get round it, so we had to keep walking alongside.

'Is this the wall?' Peter would ask again in German.

'Yes.'

'The Berlin Wall?'

'Yes.'

'The West, that's over there, is it?'

'Yes,' they'd reply.

We'd look at each other slightly confused, and they'd shrug and walk off.

The next day, still not convinced we'd seen the Berlin Wall, we planned to go across to the East again, this time overground, through the border crossing at Checkpoint Charlie. In 1945 the city of Berlin had been divided into four districts, administered by the US, France, Britain and the USSR. The West soon joined up their sectors, but there was free access to and from the Soviet sector until the Wall was built by the East German authorities in August 1961 to keep out 'Western spies and saboteurs'.

The West considered the Wall as an admission of defeat for the entire Communist system. Here now, twenty-one years later, observation platforms had been built so that you could climb up the steps and look out uneasily into the East. In marked contrast to the relatively inoffensive wall we'd seen from the other side, from the West we could see that there was not one but two walls. In the bleak, mined, one hundred yards in between the two walls stood criss-crossed anti-vehicle obstruction posts; searchlights; Alsatian dogs chained to the fence; and observation towers with the occasional glint from the binoculars of the East German guards staring back at you. In the midst of this wasteland, rabbits hopped around, going about their business, oblivious and undisturbed.

YOU ARE NOW LEAVING THE AMERICAN SECTOR warned the sign as we crossed through the turnstiles over to East Berlin. We found ourselves at an overground railway station and, as there was a train standing in the station, we got on. At about the fifth stop, I saw a poster of a big wheel.

'Here?' I asked the woman opposite. Luckily the word means and sounds the same in German.

'*Ja, Ja,*' she said, and pointed vaguely in a general direction.

'Let's go to the fair,' I said to Peter, and we got off.

We walked through a park, past a lake, and back in time to the fifties. Sitting at a café, with our staple diet of a beer and a sausage, we watched people dancing polka-like steps in pairs to an 'oompah' band. At the fairground, teenagers queued to play the slot-machines, and spin the ball-bearing to win a cigarette.

I looked up at the huge Ferris wheel. 'I've got to go on that,' I said.

We kept losing count as we watched it go round, but thought there must be about thirty carriages. I wondered if, at last, I'd found the biggest big wheel in Europe. I joined the queue and Peter went off for a wander.

In front of me were a group of seven fresh-faced teenage boys: Soviet soldiers looking smart in their khaki uniforms with red trimmings and caps. I couldn't help noticing the lengths of cotton thread hanging from the hems of their jackets. They were chatting excitedly. To the Soviet soldier, a posting to East Berlin was like a trip to Las Vegas. The queue moved quite quickly, and soon their turn came. They climbed into the circular red padded seat. The young fairground man, wearing a CND badge, counted them, and then looked at me.

'Acht!' he shouted.

He beckoned at me to get in. The soldiers looked slightly alarmed, but moved round to make room. I sat down and smiled. One of them nudged the boy sitting next to me, who nudged him back. Two boys on the other side started giggling. The CND man closed down the metal bar, and we lurched up suddenly and unsteadily. We all gave a little scream, then an embarrassed snigger. The two boys on the other side were now in uncontrollable giggles. The boy to my right was looking down and I could see his ears had turned the red of his trimmings. The other four sat and smiled at me, and I smiled back. I couldn't believe I was sitting two hundred foot up in the air on a big wheel in East Berlin with seven Soviet soldiers. It was no wonder the queue had moved so fast: the first time we arrived back at the ground, the metal bar was lifted and we had to get off. They let me out first, then all walked off towards the dodgems, pushing each other and laughing.

Peter reappeared. We didn't fancy queuing for the dodgems. Especially since it was hard to tell the difference between when they were moving at top speed and when they were slowing down to let the next lot of people get in.

Watching these soldiers, in their fraying uniforms, drive towards each other at the speed of an action replay – somehow they just didn't look to me as if they were about to invade Western Europe.

25. *Temporary Existence*

I had this degree now, but so far only my secretarial experience had been of any interest to anybody. I decided to temp until something better came up.

As a temp, you sometimes wonder whether, instead of the Brook Street Bureau, the boss had actually meant to phone Miss Whiplash or the Slappers Are Us Escort Agency. The executive may like to check on your typing by leaning, an arm either side of you, on the desk and nibbling at your neck. He may occasionally whisper about his little *pied-à-terre*, adding, 'Don't worry, I'll still fill in your time sheet.' In some jobs you're treated as the administrative equivalent of the person who's come to clean the drains, while in others, you're only there a day but you continue to meet up with those people for years to come. Other jobs just have to be put down to experience.

I was temping in a TV company that made documentaries when I was 'poached' by a man in his late thirties, named Russ, who asked me to come and work for him on a film. He was slim, not bad-looking, and could ooze a great deal of charm when he had to, so long as it was only necessary for very short periods. The film was going to be a documentary about an artist, and would involve film clips and interviews, and this sounded exactly like the kind of job I was looking for.

Our offices were on the top floor of a block of four-storey Georgian buildings near Carnaby Street. Early on in my first week, Russ was dictating some letters, when he began to tell me some painful stories about his childhood in Eastern Europe. I listened sympathetically for fifteen minutes or so to tales of what had obviously been a traumatic part of his life.

'Have you typed those letters yet?' he suddenly asked.

'No, I've been sitting here,' I said, astonished.

'You lazy cow,' he ranted, 'I don't know why I took you on,' and he promptly sacked me.

Slightly confused, I walked to my desk, collected my things, and put on my coat.

'Where are you going?' he asked.

'Home, I suppose. You just sacked me,' I replied.

'Don't be so stupid. Of course I haven't. Just get those letters typed up.'

I took off my coat, and sat back down at the typewriter.

This sequence of events would become quite a regular occurrence. Sometimes his parents would have died when he was a child; sometimes they had just died, or were about to die; and sometimes they were still alive and about to visit. I learnt early on that it was best not to contradict him, but just accept it as that morning's story. I was also sacked pretty regularly, and I'd wander off to the café on the corner, until he came to fetch me.

Russ was also currently suffering agonies from an unrequited love affair, and he talked to me about this throughout the day. As it got nearer to six o'clock, and time for me to go home, he might throw a little something into the conversation like, 'I think I might kill myself tonight.' I would end up staying there, listening to his problems, for much of the evening.

At the beginning there was also a researcher named Rob working there, so at least then we had each other to talk to for a bit of relative sanity. We would share this suicide burden between us, while trying to leave as soon as we could. Even so, Russ's possible suicide attempts were at the forefront of our minds the whole time. If he was late into the office, we had to consider what might have happened to him. Sometimes we would ring him, sometimes we would go round to his flat, sometimes we'd call the police, sometimes we would just wait for him to arrive. Only one thing was certain. Whatever course of action we took, it would obviously be the wrong one.

One evening, after Rob and I had been consoling Russ in the office for only about an hour, we were all ready to leave. Grateful for the early night, we followed Russ down the three flights of narrow stairs, and down to the big black front door. He turned the door handle but the door didn't open. It was Chubb-locked. None of us knew the door had a Chubb lock on it.

'Where's your Chubb key?' he shouted.

We wouldn't have a Chubb key, because we hadn't known there was a Chubb lock.

He started to kick the door.

'We can phone someone from one of the other offices and get them to let us out,' I suggested.

This solution was just too simple.

The solution he preferred was for us to climb out on to the roof.

'We can easily get someone to let us out,' Rob and I argued.

'No!' he yelled.

We followed him back up the stairs to the top floor, and he pulled down a rickety ladder that led out of the skylight.

'I really don't fancy this,' I said.

'Neither do I,' said Rob.

'Oh, don't be so pathetic,' said Russ and, climbing up the ladder, he started to knock open the skylight window frame with his fist. 'We can climb down into the offices next door!' he explained at maximum volume.

It wasn't just the height that Rob and I were worried about.

Russ climbed out on to the roof and, clinging on to a chimney-pot, he called us both out. We still weren't keen, but for some inexplicable reason we both climbed up the steps and out on to the roof. It was a warm summer's evening. That was the best part. I looked down, and over at the proposed route to the next skylight. It was a pitched roof. I could see no flat part to walk on whatsoever.

'I want to go back down,' I said. 'I'll sleep in the office, I don't care.'

'Don't be so stupid!' Russ yelled.

Rob climbed out.

'Bloody hell!'

Rob and I looked at each other, and our looks confirmed that we were not only worried about the height, but also about the fact that here we were, standing on a slippery roof, above a busy London street, with a man who just a few moments ago we had been trying to talk out of committing suicide. We clung on to the stack of four chimney-pots.

'We've just got to walk across to the next skylight,' said Russ. 'Come on, let's hold hands.'

Obviously, if he decided to jump, he intended to take us both with him.

'I can't do it in these shoes,' I said, clinging on to the chimney. I kicked off my high heels, which fell over the side of the building into the street. I heard them clatter down the tiles and hit the ground.

A crowd of men in white shirtsleeves outside the pub opposite looked up.

'Is there a fire?' one shouted.

'No, we're locked in!' shouted Rob.

'You don't have to tell the fucking world!' hissed Russ.

He grabbed my hand and started to edge his way across the ridge. Reluctantly, I let go of the chimney-pot and grabbed hold of Rob with the other hand. We warily edged along the ridge of the roof, with one foot on each side.

'Oh God oh God oh God,' I muttered all the way across.

The hot roof tiles forced me to reconsider the sense of throwing off my shoes. The drinkers below clutched their pints and watched in silence. A few more steps and Russ had reached the next chimney-stack. I grabbed hold and teetered round to make way for Rob.

'Help me with this thing,' said Russ as he started to lift up the neighbouring skylight. Rob grabbed one side of the frame and they lifted it up. The main excitement finished, the general hubbub resumed from the onlookers. Russ lay on the roof and tried to shake down the ladder. We watched his suntanned balding head disappear. He started to climb down the ladder, on the assumption that it would open out fully as he went down – which it didn't.

'You have to jump the last bit!' he shouted to me.

'Can you move the desk over?' I suggested.

He started to move it under the ladder, then thought better of it.

'Just bloody jump. I'll catch you!' he shouted.

I climbed to the end of the ladder, screamed, and jumped, of sorts. Russ, of sorts, caught me. I collapsed in a heap on the floor, as Rob climbed down.

We left the ladder and skylight, and started to walk down the narrow staircase.

'Let's hope they haven't got a Chubb lock as well,' I said.

We got down to the front door, it opened, and we walked out into the street.

'See!' declared Russ triumphantly, 'you weren't going to do it, were you? You thought I was mad.'

Rob soon went off to work for another company, but would often ring me to see how I was coping. The job continued in pretty much the same way, but since there had never actually been any suicide attempt, I became less and less sympathetic. I'd maybe stay half an hour later, then just leave regardless. Russ seemed at his happiest when actually filming, and for those two days, we really did have a fun time.

For a couple of weeks he employed a production manager to work out the budgets, and on her first day he talked to her about how depressed he was feeling. On her second day, it got to lunch-time and Russ still hadn't arrived. She was getting a little anxious.

'Do you think he's all right?'

'He's probably committed suicide,' I said casually.

She looked at me, shocked.

'He was talking about that only last night,' she said. 'How can you joke about it?'

'Because he's been talking about it every day I've been here,' I told her.

'Well, I think we should get someone round to his house.'

She rang the police. Russ appeared a few hours later, bellowing that because of that 'stupid cow' he'd had to get his front door fixed.

I was becoming less and less convinced that this job really was a good break into the world of film and documentary. I would come home from work shattered, and most mornings I'd throw up before I went in. My flatmates, who had to put up with most of my moaning, told me the job wasn't worth it.

One day when Russ sacked me, I picked up my coat

and bag and left. I didn't go to the café. I went home. He phoned me the next day.

'What are you playing at?'

'You sacked me,' I said.

'Course I didn't.'

'Well, I'm not coming in anyway.'

He started shouting.

'Just fuck off!' I shouted, and put the phone down.

I later found out that my six months of working for Russ had easily beaten the previous long-service record of two weeks.

26. *A London Experience*

I arrived at the offices in Piccadilly on time, and waited until the Director of Advertising came back from lunch. I'd taken the day off from temping, as I had to collect my prize. A hundred pounds was a whole week's wages for me. They were making quite a thing of it, apparently – that's why I'd dressed up. It was funny how the idea for the slogan had just come to me like that, on a crowded rush-hour bus.

Finally, a distinguished man in his fifties walked in wearing a light grey designer suit.

'This is the winner of the slogan competition,' declared the receptionist, as he glided past her desk and into his office.

'Be with you in a minute,' he called.

'He'll be with you in a minute,' repeated the receptionist.

An executive-looking woman and a young man with a

pony-tail were summoned. A man with three cameras hanging round his neck arrived at reception and announced he was there to take photos of the competition winner.

'That's me,' I told him.

This was getting exciting. I'd been told there would be publicity in all the national newspapers.

'What paper are you from?' I asked.

'The *South London Press*,' he replied.

The director reappeared and, with the words, 'Right, let's get this over with,' he strode towards the lift, followed by Pony-tail Man who was carrying a rolled-up poster.

'We're going to have a few photos of you putting a poster up in the tube,' explained the woman as she walked past, and the photographer and I leapt up and followed them to the lift. They headed towards Piccadilly. We followed to the best of our abilities, depending on what shoes we were wearing, dodging through traffic and hurtling at full speed down the steps of the tube station. The photographer gallantly lagged behind with me, on the grounds that since I was the one who was to be in the photos, there didn't seem much sense in losing me. In the underground station, the late afternoon rush hour was beginning and, as we barged through commuters and tourists, we could see the director, the woman and Pony-tail Man passing through the ticket barrier and heading down the escalator.

'They're with us,' the woman called to the ticket collector, and he let us through. Pony-tail Man now led us down a tiled corridor marked NO ENTRY to a green door at the end. It was opened by the station-manager, who invited us into a cosy old-fashioned wooden office. A man of about sixty sat wearing blue overalls covered in what can only be described as 'slop'.

'Now you're here, I'll go and get the paste made up,' he said, and went off.

'Bill will show you how to paste up the poster,' explained the station-manager. 'Is that all right?'

'Yes, that's great.'

'Do you want some overalls?'

I looked down at my new lilac dress. 'Yes, I'd better, I suppose.'

'Oh, you don't really need them,' interrupted the woman.

'This is dry-clean only,' I replied.

'We can find you some all right,' said the station-manager and, standing on his old wooden chair, he started sorting through packets of brand-new dark blue overalls on the shelf above his desk. 'Medium I guess you'd be, wouldn't you?' he continued, and handed me a plastic packet.

The executive team looked at their watches.

'I'll have to take my dress off,' I said.

They took the hint and waited outside. I quickly put on the stiff blue overalls, which would have been medium on an orang-utan, and stepped out into the growing throng of rush-hour commuters.

'That looks nice,' joked the photographer.

'If you roll the arms and legs up a bit it'll be all right,' said the station-manager with a smile on his face.

'I like them,' I said.

'Now come along, where are we doing this?' the woman demanded to know.

Born to be wild – in a refined sort of way

After the jump

(*Above left*) Stand-up look down

(*Above right*) Brushing up on some paperwork

(*Left*) With Lee Evans – looking good

(*Above*) With Jack Dee –
looking happy
(Photo credit: Fred Sanjar)

(*Left*) I quite like snakes,
actually

(*Below*) My favourite
Romanian baby

When my hair is too long for a computer
(Photo credit: Fred Sanjar)

The station-manager took us further along the corridor to a dead-end tunnel. 'We'll be out of the way here,' he said.

Bill appeared, carrying a bucket of paste and a broom under his arm. Pony-tail Man handed him the rolled-up poster.

'I'll start it off just to show you, then you can carry on,' said Bill as he dipped his broom into the bucket of paste. The executives made a quick getaway to the end of the corridor. To hold up the poster and slap on the paste at the same time definitely required skill and rhythm – and I didn't really have either. The photographer snapped away, and I dripped paste all over Bill and into my hair.

'I wouldn't take this up as a living if I was you,' laughed Bill, as he smoothed out the last few bubbles. We stood back and admired our work as the babble about budgets floated up from the other end of the tunnel.

It was the first time I'd seen my slogan displayed. WHY GO ROUND LONDON WHEN LONDON CAN GO ROUND YOU? it bellowed in two-foot-high red letters. At the very bottom of the poster in tiny letters was my name and *Winner of the slogan competition*.

'I took a couple,' the photographer said, 'but it'll probably be better if you pose.'

I held up the brush and smiled a genuinely happy smile.

The executives walked back to join us.

'Got enough?' asked Pony-tail Man.

'Yes, that's fine,' replied the photographer.

'Better take it down before it dries then.'

The station-manager stepped forward and, with one swift action, ripped the poster off the wall.

I must have looked shocked.

'We don't put posters here,' he explained quietly.

'Right, let's get back to the office!' bellowed the director, and he headed towards the escalator.

'I've got to put my dress back on,' I called out.

'Oh – you know the way back don't you? We'll see you there in a minute.'

The station-manager waited outside as I got changed in his office.

'Do you want to keep these overalls as a souvenir?' he asked.

'Oh yes, thank you.'

The photographer had finished his job now, but he was waiting for me just before the barrier.

'Tickets!'

'We haven't been anywhere,' he explained. 'We're with the advertisers.'

The ticket collector pushed us out of the way as a torrent of people spilled off the escalator. 'Get your ticket over there,' he said, pointing to Excess Fares.

'Just get a ticket,' said the photographer. 'I can claim it back.'

'They're all in there,' the receptionist told me on our return and she pointed to the director's office where a dozen or so people were crammed in, each holding a glass of champagne.

'Ah, here's our winner!' he declared as I walked in, and gave me a glass of champagne.

The other people looked round and then continued discussing client accounts. He poured the last drips of champagne into my glass. This was the last bottle, and people were beginning to drift out of his office. He sat down at his desk and started to look through some papers.

'Oh, yes, I suppose you'll be wanting this,' he said, pushing a cheque across the table to me.

'Thank you.'

'Right, that's that then.' He stood up and clapped his hands. 'Time to get on.' Amid the murmurings of meetings, the leftovers trickled out of his office. He held a cork between his thumb and finger, and leant over, close to my face. 'Would you like to keep this cork as a souvenir?' he asked slowly.

'No, I have had champagne before thanks,' I retorted, and walked out clutching my overalls.

27. *White Christmas*

For a few years Mum and I spent Christmas in various hotels, guest-houses and holiday camps around the country. We branched out from London, to places such as Torquay, Bournemouth and, one year, Margate, where so much rain leaked into the guest-house that the carpet floated off down the hallway.

These Christmas breaks are a real boom industry, and many places are booked up by the beginning of July. Each brochure title gives a clue as to what class of clientele they are trying to attract. *Bingo, Mr and Mrs Competition* or *Chirpy*

Cockney Knees-up with a Chas and Dave Tribute Band are altogether a different kettle of fish to *A Bridge Evening*, *A Visit by the Choir of St Vernon the Virtuous* and *A Boxing Day Glass of Sherry with the Wiltshire Hunt*. I don't think I need spell out where we ended up.

They all planned to start with the same Yuletide mulled-wine welcome from 'George and Vera', the 'manager and his staff' or the 'Redcoats', depending on where we went. The hosts would then find their arrangements somewhat thwarted by having to search around for a Guinness for Mum. The vast majority, in fact nearly all the people on these breaks, were women pensioners, and over the years I learnt to expect to be the youngest guest there. Occasionally there would also be just one family with small children, or a pair of lively divorcees in their forties, or a romantic young couple who had booked in for the duration. At this first festivity, warm glass in hand, they would eventually sidle up to me and say, 'I thought everyone would be a lot younger.'

I'd gaze over the roomful of identical grey-white perms and could imagine I was just above the cloud line in a plane. 'Every one I've been to has been like this,' I'd say, and together we'd nod and blow a long silent whistle.

Looking on the bright side, which I couldn't always do, I was given an insight into a different generation. I met many old-age pensioners who were as keen to spend Christmas away from their families as their families were eager not to invite them. Many had done a similar circuit of the hotels and holiday camps over the years, and would compare notes.

'You get a much better Christmas dinner at Saltdean.'

'At Eastbourne, you had your Christmas dinner in the evening.'

'Euuurghh!' they'd chorus in disgust.

Immediately on sitting down at the dinner table, someone would announce loudly, 'I've been vomiting!' – which would become the topic of conversation for the duration of the meal.

During the year of the miners' strike, a woman was telling us about her father who had worked as a miner in the thirties. The job had taken its toll on him and after a lifetime down the pit he was left with half a lung and only one kidney, but he had to carry on working because there was no sick-pay. She would see him literally crawling home up the hill from the pit, exhausted and leaning on the houses for support as he went.

'They wouldn't do that now,' she concludes, 'they're too bloody lazy.'

'You think that's how it should be then, do you?' I asked.

'The potatoes are nice, aren't they?'

'Mmm, and the carrots are lovely and fresh.'

Even though we had sets eating arrangements every day for all three meals, and rationing had been over for nigh on forty years, many guests would start to queue outside the dining room half an hour before mealtimes. Even if this meant standing outside in the rain. This would cause a dilemma for the management, who realized that if they opened the doors early, the next day the queue would form half an hour before that. As soon as you were served, an official photographer would rush around the tables taking photos of your every mouthful, to sell to you later on a light-up key-ring. Since they never asked who you were actually on holiday with, the chances of you wanting to buy a plastic souvenir of yourself and an unknown wrinkly were rather remote. I always thought that, with a little more research, they could have made a few more sales. If they managed to get us in the same photo, my mum would always buy one of us wearing metallic cardboard pointy hats, with forks full of stuffing and chipolata poised ready.

For entertainment there was: old-time dancing; talent contests; fancy dress; bitter, unknown comedians; plus the sexy-girl-with-older-greasy-bloke singing duo, called something like French Dressing. During a *The Price is Right* competition, a fake *capo di monte* ornament was given out to a lucky prizewinner. This proved to be a very popular item, and once the audience had seen them, they rushed down to the front, picked them up off the stand, and rushed back to their seats.

'No! They're the prizes!' called the MC in alarm. 'Can you bring them back, please?' he begged, to no avail.

The prizewinner, still standing on stage and holding tightly on to her ornament, asked if there was anything she could put it in so it wouldn't get broken. The hostess pulled back the curtain to reveal the distinctive cardboard boxes and an avalanche of snowy curls headed towards the stage once more. The game show was abandoned. Anarchy ruled. Truly the world had gone mad.

Concentration was at its height during the bingo sessions. If you spoke, you faced being angrily 'ssshhhed' out of the room. Mum couldn't stand bingo, and couldn't keep quiet, so when this was going on, in age-old tradition, we would make our own entertainment.

Since feeding pigeons in Trafalgar Square the first year, the feeding of some kind of bird or other was often a highlight. At Butlins in Minehead we fed the ducks that were wintering on the holiday camp's frozen swimming-pool, and in Wales we fed seagulls from our hotel balcony. Starting with the spare rolls left over from breakfast, we ended up roaming the streets of Llandudno, trying to find a shop open on Boxing Day so we could buy a sliced loaf.

Seated on the dining table behind us at Llandudno was Eric, who told us he liked children, farmyard animals and film stars. He was well over six foot tall, very bulky, but not quite all there. He had come to Butlins looking for a wife.

'Since you're the only one here under sixty-five, I suppose it'll have to be you,' he told me simply.

I thought not. He had none the less decided, unilaterally, that Mum and I would be his companions for the whole five days. My mum was happy to chat to anyone, although we would both jump when he'd suddenly thump the table for no reason. Eric would follow us around continuously, and very soon we felt he was rapidly outstaying his welcome. If we thought we'd managed to lose him, he would suddenly step out from behind a plastic potted palm-tree when we least expected it. We learnt that this ambush technique had become second nature to Eric after he'd emigrated to Australia in the sixties on a ten-pound package and, not having read the small print, ended up in the Vietnam War.

'That must have been terrible.'

'Yes,' he said seriously, 'they didn't have bingo.'

I wondered whether this could truly be termed as 'suffering'.

'One thing was easier,' he went on, 'if you wanted a woman, you just grabbed her, and that was it.'

He started to seriously give me the creeps. When we were going to our room, he'd follow us into the lift. I'd push Mum out on the wrong floor, so he wouldn't know where we were staying, then we'd walk up the stairs. After the first time, we realized it was obviously less effort to go to a higher floor and then walk down. By the fourth day, I had to ask him to leave us alone, and he said he realized I needed time to think about it.

'About what?'

'Getting married.'

In the dining room, when I ignored him, he started shouting, 'This is no way to treat your fiancé!'

28. Wires Crossed

I was living with two flatmates, Bob and Nigel, in a small block of flats in South London. Some of the tenants had been threatened by people hanging around on the stairs and had demanded that something should be done about it. The landlord agreed to install an Entryphone system. Each of the flats was provided with an impressive white phone, and each resident issued with a front-door key. We all waited for the big day with anticipation.

I arrived home after work to find a sturdy new wooden front door with brass trimmings, and alongside it a metal grille with row upon row of glowing numbered buttons. Eagerly I slid my finger across to our flat number and pressed.

'Yes?' a voice answered.

I hadn't expected a reply, and certainly not a female one.

'Is that thirty-four?' I asked.

'No, it's twenty-eight, you've pressed the wrong number.'

'I don't think I did,' I said, and pressed thirty-four again.

'Yes, that's mine!' squealed the voice. 'What happens if you press twenty-eight then?'

I decided to find out.

'Hallo?' a gruff male voice answered.

'What number are you?' I asked.

'Thirty-six. What do you want?'

'Yes!' squealed the wall. 'If you press theirs you get mine and if you press mine you get yours! What happens if you press his?'

I decided to find out.

'Who is it?' a female voice asked irritably.

'What number is that?' I asked politely.

'What number do you want?'

'Thirty-four.'

'This isn't it, you pressed the wrong number.'

'Yes, I know,' I replied, 'I pressed thirty-six.'

'What are you, blind or stupid?' it asked.

I tried to make myself heard over the other two explanations now being given.

'How many of you are there?' shouted the wall. 'I've got a sick mother up here. You wait there. I'm coming down to sort you out.'

Click, silence.

'Hallo,' I called to the wall. I realized Squeaky and Gruff had left me to my fate.

Suddenly the front door was pulled open and a haggard and harassed middle-aged woman in a flowery overall appeared. She stuck her head out of the door and glanced both ways up the street.

'Well, what are you playing at?' she asked.

I decided it would be best to keep the story brief. 'I pressed thirty-six but I got yours.'

'This is thirty-six,' she told me through gritted teeth, keeping her slippered foot in the door and her eye out for my accomplices. 'It's got it written *here*. *See?*' She emphasized every word by pressing hard on the button. Finally, a quivering voice slipped through the metal grille.

'Who is it? I was in bed?'

'Mother! What are you doing? Get back indoors.' She turned to me accusingly. 'What have you done to this thing?'

I started to explain that I was trying to get flat thirty-four.

'Here's thirty-four, here!' her bony finger darted towards the button.

'Hallo!' replied Squeaky.

'See, they're in. What are you playing at?'

'That's not thirty-four,' I explained.

'No, I'm not thirty-four,' chirped Squeaky, 'this is twenty-eight, and if you press mine you get thirty-six.'

'Thirty-six eh?' She flung herself on the button.

'No, that's yours!' I said.

'No it isn't, mine's twenty-two,' she snapped, pressing the thirty-six button once more to prove her point.

'Who is it now?' quivered the wall. 'I'd just got back into bed. I'll call the police.'

'It's all right, it's Elsie, I'm coming back up. Get back into bed, Mum.' She turned to me. 'Well the stupid bastards have obviously done the bloody thing wrong haven't they?' she said, and stormed up the stairs. I started to follow her. 'Where are you going?' she asked.

'Number thirty-four. I live there,' I replied, showing her my keys. This annoyed her even more.

'Oh for Chrissake, why didn't you use the bloody things in the first place?'

Nearly an hour later Bob arrived back in a state of bewilderment.

'That wasn't you before, was it?'

Whatever the question meant, the answer was no.

'I tied out the Entryphone and thought I got you putting on a squeaky voice, so I said, "Good evening, this is the World Service and here is the news," and this woman started squealing about the buzzers and told me to press twenty-eight, which I did and I got this miserable bloke who wasn't twenty-eight, then I pressed his number and got this woman screaming about her sick mother and threatening to come downstairs and sort me out. So I've been walking around for the last half an hour in case she was waiting for me on the stairs.'

29. Bloody Comedy

My friend John and I were wandering around Leicester Square. It was midnight, Friday, some month in 1985. The late-night film that we'd finally agreed to see was sold out, and it was too late to start the long procedure of making another cinematic hit list. Between the cinema and a Chinese restaurant was a door with a red flashing light. THE COMEDY STORE. Well, it's better than going home, we thought.

In later years, the audiences would have to queue for an hour before the doors opened to get in. This night, there was no queue and the place was half empty. I'd only vaguely heard of the mystique of the 'good old days' of the Comedy Store, but still felt excited to be in this narrow basement with its dark red painted walls. A couple of hundred plastic chairs were spread out in semi-circles from the small stage set against the wall, and opposite was the bar and more seats on a raised platform.

Naïvely, John and I sat right at the front because, strangely enough, that's where there were empty seats. There was another young couple sitting in the front row, so we left a couple of seats free and sat to their right. They had that uneasy air of being on a first date, and the young man looked as though he was out to make an impression. He was wearing a suit and could have come straight from the Statement Enquiries counter. By the time the second comic came on stage he had plucked up a bit of courage. He also had that uneasy air of being on his first heckle.

'Shut up!' he called out.

This stopped the comic in his tracks, since he'd not heard such a pathetic heckle in a very long time. He looked down at this specimen sitting right in front of him, and laughed. '*You* shut up!' he replied.

Obviously stumped now, the young man left it a while to regroup his thoughts. A few minutes later, with a confident nod to his date, he called out again. 'Go on, shut up!'

The comic drastically upped the stakes with, 'Piss off, you sad wanker!'

Angrily, the young man hurled his beer up into the comic's face.

The comic picked up his own drink and emptied the glass of beer over the punter, who was by now desperate to save his rapidly diminishing chance of a second date. He grabbed the bottom of the mike stand and started to pull. The comic grabbed the top half. 'Let go, you wanker!' he shouted. But wanker wouldn't let go, and the mike stand was pulled backwards and forwards in true heave-ho fashion. 'Well, if you want it so bad, you can have it,' said the comic, and let go.

Wanker pulled the mike stand back, straight smack into his girlfriend's face. She screamed and blood spattered along the row towards us. The young man was on his feet, jumping this way and that, torn between protecting his girlfriend and thumping the comic. The girl was sobbing and angrily pushed him away, so, that choice blocked, he got on stage. Half a dozen people immediately went to the girl's aid, and the manager ran to the front of the stage. The comic was distraught. Still fending off the boyfriend, he was trying to see if the girl was all right, and now he had the manager's anger to contend with too. For whatever reason I went towards the side of the stage and grabbed the manager's arm. 'It wasn't the comic's fault!' I said.

The compère went on to try to calm down the situation, and called an interval. An ambulance was called and the second half of the show went on as normally as it could.

30. *Cockalooney*

While I was temping, and hoping that a job other than secretarial would somehow turn up, I started to go to some drama evening classes I'd seen advertised in a library. They were run by a formidable Greek-Australian woman called Effie, who inspired and frightened the dozen of us into doing whatever tasks or games she set.

She did not rely on volunteers, which suited me, because I never volunteered for anything. Everybody had to do every exercise or else leave the class, and my heart would thump in terror when it got close to my turn.

In the first class, she told me to stand on a chair at one end of the old schoolroom, and got a girl called Fiona to do the same at the other end.

'You are the stone lions in Trafalgar Square,' she told us. 'Now, what would you talk about?'

I knew I didn't speak very loud, and I really thought I was going to faint and fall off the chair. I started to moan about the pigeons.

'This lion can't hear you,' Effie called from the far end of the room.

In terror, I started shouting about pigeons and Nelson and traffic and tourists and bird shit *ad nauseam*.

These two hours on a Friday evening kept me going through times when everything else seemed to be going nowhere.

Fiona was a student at London University, and was soon going off for three weeks to the Edinburgh Festival, an event that was now slightly more familiar to me. They had had trouble casting one part in the play and she suggested that I go along to a rehearsal.

'But I don't go to London University,' I said.

'Just say you do,' she said, 'they won't know.'

So I ended up at the Edinburgh Festival after all, in a bizarre, rarely seen Tennessee Williams play, performing the part of the Cockalooney Bird. My role was to run about on stage squawking.

'When?' I asked.

'Whenever you want.'

The play went very well – a cockalooney bird was at least one step up from my previous role as a red ant – but, although only Fiona and I knew it, my best performance was pretending to be the London University student. In the second week, we thought it was safe to own up.

Someone else in Effie's class told me about the British Theatre Association, so, instead of going on holiday, I went on their summer course in Cheltenham. I arrived the first evening to find three hundred people, two hundred and ninety-two of whom were twenty years older than me. Is this what people mean when they say they hang around with an older crowd? I wondered. The eight of us of a similar age immediately banded together, and then found that most of the others weren't too bad either. The course started early in the morning, went on till late at night, and the socializing began after that.

On the first day I met James, who wanted to be an actor, and it was love at first sight. At the end of the course I was given the lead in one of the plays, and I decided there and then that I wanted to be an actress. They may not have been *Ten Days That Shook the World*, but they had certainly shaken up my life.

The band of eight of us decided to stay for an extra night, and we all went out to a restaurant. We had been totally inspired by this course, and were all going to give up our jobs and enter showbiz. The time it took for this feeling to wear off varied among us – and for some of us it didn't wear off.

At the end of the meal, everyone gave me their cheques and money, and I was going to pay on my credit card. The waiter took a while to return and, as we sat around, Bill suddenly made a stupid face and we all laughed. I carried on laughing after the others had stopped.

'It wasn't *that* funny!' they said, as tears streamed down my face.

'I know!' I shrieked, but I couldn't do anything about it. I slid off my chair and under the table. A couple of people pulled me out, and the waiters came over, quite anxious now that we should leave.

'I'm not drunk!' I squealed, and I wasn't.

They plonked me back on the seat, but I was still giggling. The waiters brought the bill, and the credit-card slip. I tried to sign it, but my hand was so limp after all the giggling I couldn't write. They came back with another slip. I made some mark across it, which they couldn't accept. I carried on giggling, as everyone took their money back and hastily started to write out new cheques.

I was just starting to calm down when Bill, thrilled at his audience reaction, made the stupid face again. I shrieked and James thought it was time to take me outside for some fresh air. Outside I was no better. I fell giggling across a car bonnet and the alarm went off, which made me even worse. James started to gently slap my face. I couldn't stand up. The others came out and James and Bill helped me along the street on my rubbery legs back to the bed and breakfast where we were staying.

'Ssh,' James whispered as he tried to open the front door and prop me up with the other arm at the same time.

I howled with laughter, even though by now it was hurting.

'Ssh!'

He tried to drag me up the stairs, as I giggled past the feet of the landlord coming out of his room.

'Is she drunk?' he asked.

'No, I think she's a bit tired,' replied James.

'Well, try and keep the noise down.'

We got to the room, and I crawled in and lay giggling

on the floor. James knelt down. I looked at his face. He looked so frightened, I immediately stopped. I'd been giggling for nearly two hours.

When we came back James moved into my room at the South London flat and we wrote off for auditions in fringe-theatre productions. Just buying the actors' newspaper *The Stage* felt exciting enough. We also started going to a Drama evening class. Suddenly, the temping didn't seem quite so bad.

'Profit share', I got to learn, was an optimistic term, which meant that if you were lucky you got nothing and if you were unlucky you had to chip in to help pay for the loss. I must have been very lucky in my first play, *Chicken* (keeping to my animal theme), because I was paid twenty-five pounds after a month of pretty good audiences.

After that first trip to the Comedy Store, I joined Kit Hollerbach's classes there on a Saturday afternoon. These were called Improvisation classes, and this is when I first heard the term and realized that this was what we had been doing with Effie. Kit was also a good teacher and also didn't wait for volunteers. Among the people in her class were Paul Merton and Julian Clary, who had been doing the comedy circuit for a couple of years, and Mike Myers, later to become famous in the film *Wayne's World*.

31. Comedy One Two Three

I wrote my first five minutes of stand-up in May 1986, moments after I'd thrown James's belongings out of the window. He'd met someone new on holiday. Having been the catalyst for my acting, he inadvertently became the catalyst for my stand-up, even though none of the material was about him.

On Thursday 10 July 1986 I went with a friend, Flavia, to a fledgling comedy club in the bar of a small theatre in Highgate, North London. There were about fifty people in the audience, and just before the interval the compère announced that anyone could get up in the second half and do a try-out spot. I wondered about the five minutes of material I had written, which was in my drawer at home. Maybe I could remember that. I thought about it and talked it over with Flavia. She said I should have a go. I went to the bar and downed four double Southern Comforts and lemonade.

The compère called out my name, I walked on stage, and talked about being a secretary and an only child. From what I can remember, it went down quite well.

'I bet I was really gabbling, wasn't I?' I asked Flavia.

'No, you were talking really slow.'

'It didn't feel slow in my head.'

Two men wearing Bermuda shorts introduced themselves as the Beach Bullies, and asked me to do their club in a fortnight's time.

The second-ever gig was at the Comedy Store a week

later, at three in the morning. The act before me was a young man wearing a white dinner-suit and black bow-tie who walked elegantly on to the stage, and said absolutely nothing. The audience stared at him, then started shouting. He took out of his pocket a large bottle of tomato sauce, unscrewed the cap, leant his head back, and up-ended the bottle into his mouth. The contents dripped in, hurried along only slightly by him occasionally hitting the bottom of the bottle. Slowly he lifted his head until he was facing the audience. His cheeks were puffed and full. Purposefully, from his inside pocket, he took out a plastic gun, placed it to his head, fired, and spat tomato sauce all over the audience. He fell down 'dead' on the stage.

A few people at the back laughed, the people at the front shouted, and the rest got up to leave. The compère rushed on while there was still an audience and introduced me. I didn't take my coat off because I thought I might not be stopping long. I walked on and said my act into a microphone for the first time. I didn't get heckled, more ignored than anything. The remaining twenty or so people were either still engrossed in cleaning themselves up or lying slumped over the tables. During my act, the Sauce Man climbed out from between my legs, and stumbled off the stage.

The third gig was the show I'd been booked for by the Beach Bullies, on a Saturday lunch-time at a pub in Islington. I now had my name mentioned in the listings section of *Time Out* magazine as:

'Hattie Hayridge – I've got absolutely no idea who she is.'

After the gig, which was recorded as 'quite good' in my

new notebook, I was given ten pounds, and a man named Fred came up and asked if he could take my publicity photos.

This was getting Big Time.

32. Play Thing

In 1986 I performed at the well-known Edinburgh Festival for a week in a 'loss-share' play advertised in the back of *The Stage*. The group finally settled at seven people, and we rehearsed solidly for about five months. For nearly all of this time, we did not see a script, but rehearsed anyway by breathing, chanting, walking around the room and rolling around on the floor. Some of the actors had nowhere to live so they'd moved into a derelict pub in the London Docklands, which we started to use for rehearsals. A month before we were due to go to Edinburgh and leave this pub, we were charged with squatting and ordered to appear in the High Court in the Strand, a fairy-tale castle of a building that, in other circumstances, I'd always wanted to see inside. Our director conducted our defence, and the elderly judge seemed to be rather thrilled by the whole idea. 'So you're all actors,' he said. 'How marvellous. I think you should stay there until you put on your show,' and he awarded costs against the property company.

The director decided that the set for the play should be made up of nine bags of earth from Epping Forest, which we dug up and drove to Edinburgh in a Transit van.

'Why can't we dig up some earth when we get there?' I asked.

Apparently it made all the difference to the feel of the play, to take Earth lovingly gathered from Home rather than any old earth that we dug up when we arrived. Somehow, after all these months of rehearsal, this argument appeared not only plausible, but very strong. The posters, all five of them, were produced individually with gold paint and lovingly decorated with potato print. We had about a dozen smaller versions of the poster as leaflets, which we'd have to ask people to read and then give back. In Edinburgh, we shared a flat, where we alternated sleeping in the bed with sleeping on the floor. We performed our play in a gym, and our audience ranged that week from two to the heady heights of five in number. We all went our separate ways after Edinburgh. There had been ups and downs, and the whole half year had seemed a bit mad.

A few months later I received a hefty pile of papers through the post that turned out to be a psychology thesis. This document, written by our director, set out the process of getting together a group of people and showing what you could make them do, in the guise of putting on a play at the Edinburgh Festival.

33. Getting On

While I was in Edinburgh doing the 'play', two comics from Kit's class were running a cabaret called 'The Port Stanley Amateur Dramatic Society', and said I could do five minutes each night of the second week. This turned out to be the club where most of the comics hung around. I got to meet them, and they got to see me and recommend me to clubs on the circuit back in London.

My first taste of fame was one Monday morning in early 1987, when I walked into an office to start a temp job. As I sat down, a man in a suit pointed and yelled at me from another desk. 'I recognize you!'

'I haven't been here before,' I said.

'No, not from here!' he yelled excitedly. 'I saw you on Saturday night. On stage in Catford.'

Two thoughts clashed in my head. The first was: How embarrassing; the second: Time to give up the day job.

I started to organize myself. The secretarial skills came in useful for typing out my act for every gig, and I sent off my publicity photos, taken by Fred. At a jumble sale, I bought a black-and-white striped dress, either from the twenties or the sixties, I never quite knew which, and decided that this would be my stage dress.

Malcolm Hardee's Tunnel Club on a Sunday night was a notorious venue. It was the rowdiest, roughest and most exciting club on the circuit. Nestling between the south entrance to the Blackwall Tunnel and an industrial estate, the smell of the Tate & Lyle sugar factory outside could only be matched by the smell of frightened performer on the inside. The atmosphere was like the Wild West. Being on stage was like hanging on to a bucking bronco and seeing how long you could stay on for.

I was on stage when a man came out from the toilets and started taking a short cut across the back of the stage. He walked up behind me and lifted my stripy dress up over my head. I don't know if it was the shock or the embarrassment, but I saw red and landed him a well-aimed kick in the groin and carried on kicking him all the way back to his seat. The audience laughed and cheered as, calming down from my hot flurry, I went back to the mike and carried on with my act. After a couple of minutes, something that felt like a cricket ball hit me in the face. Either it had numbed the nerve endings to my ears, or the room had gone quiet. I lifted my hand to my cheek and wiped away the egg that was running down from my eye. It had been thrown by the man who had lifted up my dress. I walked over to where he was sitting and, lifting up a tray full of glasses from a nearby table, stood over him. I held the tray a few inches above his head, thinking through the consequences of smashing it down over his head. He was saved as much by my indecisiveness as anything. I decided maybe not, walked back to the mike, said, 'Good night,' and walked off.

Malcolm wandered back on stage, and gallantly asked the audience, 'Who thinks we should chuck this bloke out?'

I expected them to say, 'Nah, stupid cow,' but I'd

underestimated their sense of chivalry. 'Yes!' went up one cry, followed by yells of 'Out of order', and 'Bang out of order', and a couple of blokes grabbed the man and dragged him out through the mob, throwing pints of beer in his face as they went, and out of the door. I managed to land him a girly punch on his way past.

Well, that's that over, I thought, as my right eye started to swell, but Malcolm reintroduced me on to the stage to carry on with the act. A few one-liners later, with my eye closing up rapidly, I said, 'I'm getting off now. I feel a bit dizzy.'

'What did you get off for?' asked the bloke at the bar. 'You were doing really well.'

In February 1987, I was doing a five-minute open spot at a club in Twickenham called the Bearcat. I'd just met someone who had been telling me all about my ex and his new girlfriend, so, emotionally, it had not been a good day. When I got into the kitchen/dressing-room, which led on to the stage, it was already crowded with the producers of a new show called *Saturday Night Live*, who were there to watch a comic called Harry Enfield.

I started into my act and three women at the front started maliciously joining in, very quietly, at the end of everything I said.

'Did you? Is it? Really! How interesting.'

Senses are very acute while on stage – and you can hear people talking about you, even if they are whispering. You can mistakenly assume that everyone else in the room can hear them as well. I made some remark to these women that must have come totally out of the blue for 99 per cent of the people there. A two-tone 'Ooooooooo' went up from the audience, and they started to make cat meow noises, until they were louder than me. I said good night, walked off stage, hit my head on the door frame, stepped back into the kitchen, and burst into tears.

A comic named Ben Elton came up to me.

'Don't get upset about it,' he said sympathetically.

'I'm not,' I cried.

'Don't cry,' he said, 'you had some good jokes there.'

'I'm not crying,' I cried.

'No,' he agreed, and went through a few of the lines with me. 'That was a good one, and your mum and the Queen.' Mascara and tears were pouring down my face and dripping off the end of my chin. 'Do you want to go into the other bar?' he asked, probably because, as much as anything else, I must have been putting off the other performers. Although I can't remember this bit, we must have walked through the audience and round into the other side of the pub. After I had recovered, we came back round and watched the rest of the show.

Saturday Night Live and its successor, *Friday Night Live*, with Ben Elton, became the best and most popular stand-up show made to date, and Harry Enfield became a star first as Stavros, then as Loadsamoney.

My mum told people that I had started working at night in clubs. She could never tell the difference between cars, even before they became indistinguishable, so when I got an old Wolseley with wing mirrors she mistakenly told people I'd got a Rolls-Royce. Some people, on receiving these two snippets of information, had begun to draw the wrong conclusions.

When I went home one Sunday lunch-time, my mum asked, 'Do you take your clothes off on stage?'

'No,' I replied, 'I tell jokes.'

'That's all right then,' she said, then dished up the roast potatoes.

I thought that maybe she should come and see me in a show. I chose one at the Hackney Empire, where she came with my Aunt Lil.

'Don't some of them swear!' she said.

This is what I'd been a bit concerned about. The swearing, and my jokes about her.

'I should get 10 per cent for the jokes about me,' she said.

It was Friday 8 April 1988, and Mum had told her friends at the pub that I was going to be on the telly. Despite, I think, not being 100 per cent certain of the reliability of this news, Ron had rigged up a set in the bar. People who had never seen this show before, and who would probably never watch it again, stood round with their pints of bitter. The longer it went on, the more their doubt began to filter through.

'Are you sure she's on, Lil?' they'd ask, half smiling.

'Yes, she said she is.'

'She was having you on.'

'No,' my mum insisted. 'She is on it.'

Josie Lawrence appeared in a sketch.

'Is that her?' someone asked.

'No, she's blonde.'

Adverts came and went.

Julian Clary appeared.

'That's not her, is it?' someone laughed.

A blonde singing duo appeared.

'No, she's on her own.'

Annie Lennox appeared.

'No, she's not singing.'

Adverts came and went again.

'Please welcome Hattie Hayridge!'

'There's Janie!' shouted Mum.

'She's bloody good, mate,' they said after my five minutes of jokes, and everybody came up and gave her a hug.

I was so excited to be on the show, and *Friday Night Live* was one of my best and favourite gigs ever.

'Feeling a bit better tonight?' Ben smiled.

34. *A Parallel Universe*

Red Dwarf, for the uninitiated, is a comedy series set in space. It is shown at irregular intervals on BBC2 Television throughout a lot of this world and quite possibly a few others.

'Red dwarf.'

'Red wolf.'

'No, "dwarf". Red. Dwarf. Red dwarf.'

'Uh?'

'Red dwarf. As in dwarf, little person.'

'Like a midget, you mean?'

'Yes.'

'Is there a dwarf in it?'

'No.'

'Oh.'

For a few months in 1988, I'd acquired an agent who had no faith at all in what was being called 'alternative comedy'. Leaning back in his red leather chair, he would take a long puff on his cigar, then suddenly lean forward, thump the desk and shout, 'Come on, darling, it's all students! It's all rooms above pubs! You can't go around playing the f*ck*ng Fart and F*ck It all your life!' (Presumably one of the chain of Firkin pubs.)

The script of 'Parallel Universe' was sent to me, care of this agent, and I was asked to appear in this last episode of the second series of *Red Dwarf*. In this story, the crew of the spaceship discover a universe where most of the male characters find their female equivalents. I was asked to play Hilly, the female to Norman Lovett's computer, Holly. The executive producer was Paul Jackson, who had directed the hit series *The Young Ones*, and was the most hip man to be working with. He'd apparently seen me on *Friday Night Live* and put my name forward for the show.

I already knew Norman from the pub and club comedy circuit, and had done a few gigs with him. In fact, my first proper review had described me as 'a female Norman Lovett', because we both had a slow deadpan delivery, so

I guess this had something to do with why they chose me for 'Parallel Universe'.

Since this was the second series of *Red Dwarf*, it meant only one series had been shown on television, and of that I'd only seen a bit of one episode. Norman and I met up, chatted about the part, I went home with his videos of the first series, and became an immediate fan.

On the morning of Tuesday 21 June 1988, I walked out of the tube station at North Acton, West London. I had first gone, unnecessarily in my panic, to North Ealing, West London then West Acton, West London before my compass had blown a fuse. How pleased, excited and relieved I was, eventually, to walk into the BBC rehearsal rooms, a building that on any other occasion might have struck me as an ugly seventies concrete office block. In reception the first taste of showbiz was the black plastic board, with its white plastic letters spelling out the names of the shows being rehearsed. Since some of the letters had dropped off, you could have been forgiven for thinking you'd stumbled across a Polish language class.

I went through the swing-doors of the *Red Dwarf* rehearsal room, and was immediately introduced to the cast: Craig Charles, Chris Barrie, Danny John-Jules and, of course, Norman. I'd seen Craig once at the Comedy Store, but I didn't know Danny or Chris at all. The writers, Rob Grant and Doug Naylor, were there, and Ed Bye, the producer and director. I sidled over to Norman.

'Exciting innit,' I said.

'Yes, you'll enjoy yourself,' he nodded knowingly.

As all the regular cast had their parallel universe equivalents, this was a full week as far as guests were concerned. The large rehearsal room itself was painted white, with strip-lighting in the ceiling, and windows all along one wall. There were lengths and squares of coloured bits of gaffer tape stuck all over the floor. Had I been a person with an abnormal obsession for tidiness, I might have picked them up and put them in the bin. This would have been a mistake, because these bits of tape were mapped out to the exact size and shape of the sets that we would use three days later in the TV studio.

We found enough chairs for all of us, then sat round in a circle to read through the script. Ed then worked through the scenes, rehearsing them with the cast, first with the scripts, then without, gradually plotting out where everyone would stand and where they would move to.

Since we did not yet have the real objects, all manner of things were used to represent the props. In the rehearsal room there were a couple of netball posts, which could be anything from a door to a monster; as well as babies' building blocks; litter-bins; plastic coffee cups; shopping bags; and an assortment of bric-à-brac. At times, it seemed harder for the cast to remember what prop they were using than what lines they should be saying.

'Sorry, the gun. Is that the banana or the toilet-roll holder?'

On Friday morning there was a technical run-through, which meant the main lighting and sound engineers, the set and costume designers, prop-makers, cameramen, and special effects people watched a run-through of the episode, so they could work out how best to do their own job. On

Friday afternoon, we all got the plane up to Manchester where the show would be recorded.

On Saturday we went over to the BBC studios to rehearse in and around the actual sets. It was the first time I'd seen the ship and the sleeping quarters, and I felt like some overgrown Goldilocks wandering around, testing out the chairs and the bunk-beds.

'Ooh, and this one's just right.'

Sunday meant more rehearsal, followed by the dress rehearsal. This was a run through the whole episode with everyone wearing their costumes, although Danny generally ran around in a dressing-gown with his hair in curlers. Norman's costume was a black polo-neck jumper and, therefore, since I was his female copy, so was mine. The two of us looked like a couple of beatniks in search of an existential jazz band. We were then ready for the make-up department. My hair, already in a bobbed style, was turned under with the curling-tongs and sprayed solidly to keep it there. Norman and I stood closely together in front of our black background and, through the wonders of technology, appeared to be talking to the others on the computer screen.

It had been fun being in this show, and as far as I knew this was to be my only journey on the *Red Dwarf* spaceship. Like the TV audience, I would have to wait until October to see what the episode looked like.

The next day I went off to the Just for Laughs Comedy Festival in Montreal (against the advice of my agent, who couldn't find it in his *A–Z of London*).

35. Candid Canada

I'd had a long time to get excited about performing at the 1988 Montreal Comedy Festival because I'd been invited just after the previous one ended. In 1987, I'd been spotted at the well-known Edinburgh Festival.

That year I shared a flat there with Steve, a stage-manager who I'd met a couple of times before. The flat had two bedrooms, one on the ground floor and one up a wooden ladder in the attic room. Steve asked if I'd mind having the one in the attic because, as he was well over six foot tall, he wouldn't be able to get through the hatch, or stand upright if he did get up there.

The first morning, just as it was getting light, I woke up in the attic room and saw Steve's head appearing at the hatch.

'What's the matter?' I asked.

He didn't reply, but continued climbing up the ladder.

'Steve,' I called.

I could see almost all of Steve by now, and all that I could see was naked. He stepped off the top of the ladder, and started walking slowly towards me. I pulled the duvet tight up round my neck.

'Steve!' I shrieked.

Steve blinked and looked at me.

'Where am I?' he asked.

'In my room.'

He looked around. Then looked down.

'Sorry!' he said, trying to cover himself with his hands.

'Oh God, sorry!' Half crouching, and wholly panicking, he tried to make his way backwards towards the ladder. 'Sorry!' He climbed back down.

I leapt out of bed, closed the hatch, dragged the dressing-table across on top of it, then wrote a note to a friend, starting with the words, 'In case anything happens to me . . .' I emerged from my room at nearly lunch-time, when I thought Steve might have gone out, but he was sitting in the kitchen.

'Do you want a fry-up?' he asked nervously.

I wasn't sure.

'I'm sorry about all that this morning,' he said, embarrassed. 'I should have warned you. I sometimes sleepwalk when I stay in a strange place.'

We sat down and had our fry-up, and I tore up the letter to my friend, although I did continue dragging the dressing-table over the hatch until well into the third week.

The Montreal Festival lasted nearly ten days, but I was going a fortnight before and staying a fortnight after, just to be on the safe side. They allowed performers two air tickets so they could take their agent, spouse, lover, friend, double bass or the woman from the airport duty-free. I took my friend, Flavia, and we intended to do a bit of travelling around Canada both before and after the festival. In the first two weeks, we'd planned to get the train across to Vancouver, staying a while at the Rockies on the way, then get the train back in time for the start. The Canadian travel agent found this idea quite amusing.

'You realize it's further to Vancouver than it is to England, don't you?'

We didn't. So that was out.

The first few days in Montreal I spent working out what language changes would be needed in my act. I had it all typed out, and the organizers read it to see if there were any bits that North Americans wouldn't understand. I only needed to do ten minutes of material, so I thought it best to leave out jokes that would need too many words changing, otherwise I wouldn't know what I was talking about myself. I tried out the act in a couple of clubs in Montreal, plus one in Toronto, as Flavia and I travelled around. With minor changes, it seemed to be a fairly universal type of act.

'Do you have this? Do you know what this means? What do you say for this?'

I've since found that the sound check time, of about two hours, can be easily used up by asking technicians these sort of questions. They are usually very keen to help out, because if they have suggested something, they can be as eager as the comic to see how the audience responds.

Flavia and I settled for travelling mostly around Quebec, a province that on its own is bigger than Britain, and got a train to Gaspé, nearly five hundred miles away. To save our money, we self-consciously checked into a youth hostel, and immediately wished we hadn't when two coachloads of Belgian school kids turned up. As we sat outside on a bench, in the evening sun, the two coach drivers asked us if we fancied going into the nearest town to see if there was anything happening. We thought, rather than just wait for our turn to use the draughtboard, we might as well. I honestly can't remember the names of the coach drivers so, for the sake of convenience, I'll call them Hank and Chuck.

We headed into town in one of the 52-seater coaches, and wandered into a couple of bars and one restaurant, and were the only four people in each of them.

'What's the longest you've been asleep at the wheel?' Hank asked Chuck by way of conversation.

'About half an hour. One of the passengers woke me up because we'd gone past the services.'

When we got back to the coach to leave, Chuck realized he had left the lights on, and the battery was flat.

'Shit,' he said, 'we'll have to bump-start it.'

Flavia and I looked at each other. Bump-start a 52-seater coach?

Chuck took the handbrake off and, without any lights and taking up the whole of the main street, we coasted down the hill into darkness. It still didn't start, and we sat in the dark coach on a bend in the road.

'We'll have to stay here then,' said Hank, half joking.

'We can get a cab,' I said, as Flavia and I were now quite anxious to call a halt to the evening.

Some headlights appeared in the road in front of us, and a small Citroën 2CV trundled towards us. Chuck waved down the driver. 'Got any jump-leads?' he asked.

Flavia and I laughed. He couldn't be serious. He was. Chuck connected the two batteries and, as the coach flickered into life, the car died.

'They're home anyway,' said Hank, as we drove off back to the hostel.

We made it back to Montreal the day before the festival, just as the other comedians started to arrive. As we strode back into the hotel in our rags and rucksacks, we felt as if we'd been there for months already. The festival was great fun. I'd had good mentions in the reviews; one even said that I stole the show. Standing on stage, performing to an audience of three and a half thousand enthusiastic people, was the most fantastic feeling.

For the following fortnight Flavia and I travelled around again, staying with Flavia's godfather in New York while I did my act at two clubs, Carolines and Catch a Rising Star.

The first time I travelled on the New York subway, a man jumped on and called out, 'Is this going to 42nd Street?'

No one answered.

'Just because I'm black, none of you white mother-f*****s are going to answer me, is that right?'

No one answered. Pause. He glared around the carriage. I was standing quite close to him, and thought he deserved my explanation at least.

'Well, I didn't answer,' I piped up, 'because I'm lost, and I don't know where it's going.'

'Hey lady!' he screamed. 'Where did you get that accent?'

'England.'

'You from England? Wow, that's funny.' He got off at

the next stop, laughing. 'I like you, lady.' Then he shouted, 'But I still hate the rest of you motherf★★★★★s!'

36. Smile

If you perform well on television, you hope that everyone saw it. If it goes badly, you hope the transmitter got struck by lightning and knocked out the TV channel for the whole country. Some gigs that are bad at the time can become one of the best, as far as retelling the story goes. Other gigs send shivers down your spine every time you think of them, and you hope that by telling people the background story they won't think as badly of you as they otherwise might.

My very worst gig, which has not, and I'm sure never will, improve in my mind with the passing of years, took place in October 1988. I was asked, and I agreed to do, a free benefit gig in aid of hurricane damage in the West Indies. The show, I was told over the phone, was to be a mixture of comedy and music, largely from bands of the calibre of Robert Palmer and U2. I was phoned again and told that the show would be at the Dominion Theatre in the West End. The next time I was phoned about it I was told it would be shown on Channel 4 Television; and the last phone call combined all the previous information, but added that it would be shown on television, live.

I was told to be at the theatre for a sound check at eleven o'clock on the Sunday morning of the show. Since I was performing in Swansea on the Saturday night, this meant staying up to get a train at about four in the morning, going home for a bath, programming the video, then going straight to the theatre. I got there in time for eleven o'clock and waited. Despite the fact that a comic pretty much only has to say, 'One, two,' into a mike for a sound check, there apparently wasn't time for me to do this at eleven o'clock, or at any other time that day. So, with no rehearsal or sound check, I was going to do five minutes in a 3,000-seater theatre that would be shown live on television.

After waiting nearly ten hours in the wings of the Dominion Theatre, which was packed with people, most of whom had queued up overnight to see U2, I was eventually told what was going to happen. Just before I was to start, the viewers at home would be watching a three-minute film of the storm damage, along with footage of how their money would be helping the cause. This film would not be shown in the theatre, so I was told to walk on stage and wait for a member of the crew to signal that the TV film had finished.

'OK, go! go! go!' shouted someone as they pushed me on to the stage. I didn't actually need pushing – the theatre at Montreal had held three and a half thousand people, and I'd felt excited there, not scared. What I did need in front of this size audience though, and what wasn't there, was a stand with a mike in it. Someone rushed on and gave me a hand-held radio mike. Unfortunately, my best joke involved waving my arms. I'll just have to wave the one arm, I thought. Although the TV audience at home were watching the hurricane film, I was standing there doing nothing in front of three thousand people. I looked around, trying to find where this person might be whose vague signal I was supposed to spot in an auditorium of that size, and couldn't see anything at all. The audience were getting restless. A chant started up. 'U2, U2, U2.'

I wondered how far they were through the film on the television. Eventually, a woman in the audience, absolutely nothing to do with the technical crew, shouted, 'Tell us a joke, love!'

So I did. I told a couple of what were usually my best jokes, including the one where I had to awkwardly wave one arm instead of two. But the chanting grew, and I hastily came to the end of my couple of minutes, said, 'Good night,' and walked off stage.

'Great, great, that was great!' said the first person in the wings.

'It wasn't, it was shit!' I replied angrily. Unfortunately, I hadn't realized just quite how shit it was. 'Had the film finished when I started my routine?' I asked someone watching the TV back stage.

'What film?' he asked.

'The film showing all the storm damage.'

'There wasn't any film,' he replied.

He was right. I paid my taxi fare home to see on video what millions of people had been watching live. The TV audience had seen the same as the three thousand people in the theatre, which was me standing there, staring into space for thirty seconds.

As a few gigs were cancelled over the next couple of months, I wished I'd said something like, 'U2 have left the building,' and caused a mass riot, and been remembered for that rather than for looking like a rabbit trapped in the car headlights.

37. *Monkey Rock*

One cold wet depressing late afternoon on a Tuesday in January, I walked into Thomas Cook's.

'Where can I go tomorrow?'

The woman looked through the computer.

'We've got Gibraltar!' she exclaimed, speaking as a travel agent rather than a patriot.

The plane came in to land as gusts of wind and rain pushed us ever nearer to the dark, looming Rock. Lower and lower until, unexpectedly, we'd taken off again.

'This is your captain speaking. I'm sorry – we're experiencing weather difficulties. We're just going to try that again.'

Down, down, the plane swooped, swaying from side to side, rain lashing against the windows. This time, as we neared land, I could see a line of luminous tombstones standing by the side of the runway. Down, down, down, then higher and higher. Whimpers could be heard from among the passengers.

'Sorry about that, ladies and gentlemen – we're just going to have one more try.'

One more? Then what?

Our final descent then, in the rain, the darkness, the gale, the thunder, and in the lightning now bleaching the tombstones brilliant white. Nearer, nearer, third time lucky, an inch above the runway, almost touching that glistening tarmac, and up! up! we were on our way again.

No announcement this time, just an eerie silence, as if the pilot knew we were all just a tiny bit vexed with him. A few more minutes and we learnt that, far from sulking in his cockpit, he'd obviously been frantically phoning around.

'I'm afraid the storm is too strong for us to land at Gibraltar, we will be travelling on to Tangiers.'

Good, I thought, I've never been to Tangiers. I'd never been to Gibraltar either, but Tangiers sounded so much more exotic. Also, I'd never been to Faro in Portugal, when his next announcement told us we were landing there, and I'd never been to Malaga in Spain, when we did eventually land there. How much safer was it, I wondered a few hours later, being driven a hundred miles along a dark, mountainous road in a thunderstorm, by a convoy of elderly sleepy bus drivers who had all been woken up in the middle of the night.

Every one of the four days I was in Gibraltar, I would walk up to the top of the Rock with a carrier bag full of satsumas and feed the monkeys. This made a nice healthy change for them, not to be fed the chocolate and cough sweets I'd seen other people giving them. I would throw the satsumas, one by one, and watch the monkeys peel and eat them for an hour or more every day. I liked to think I had some understanding of monkeys. The big ones expect to be fed first in the natural hierarchy of things, but since humans tend to feed the little ones, we probably cause havoc in the group. I tried to be fair and fed the little ones while the big ones were occupied.

On my last day I went up to the Rock, and as I walked up the last bit of the hill, the monkeys came running to meet me. Oh, that's so sweet, I thought, they recognize me. A little one leapt on to the hem of my dress and swung round on it. How cute. Another held on to my handbag strap, and I just managed to hold on to it that bit tighter. Just high spirits. Half a dozen came running towards me. I was beginning to get a little bit worried. Four of them started pulling at the carrier bag. One of them ripped it and some of the satsumas fell out on to the ground. I tried to save the rest from falling out, but a monkey was swinging round on my coat. I tried to brush him off. It wasn't easy – monkeys are not like flies you can brush off. More were coming towards me. I started to panic. I ripped open the rest of the carrier bag and threw it away from me. The monkeys made for it, and I walked back down the hill. The little bastards!

Just give us the bloody satsumas, woman . . . keep pissing about . . . one at a time. That's what they'd been thinking.

38. Casbah Camels

Since Tangiers had proved to be so teasing on the flight over, I booked a day trip from Gibraltar. The minibus didn't pick up passengers from my hotel so I had to wait for it at The Holiday Inn up the road. I got there early so I could lounge around with a cappuccino and a few croissants.

As I handed my bus ticket to the driver, a woman's northern accent bombarded me.

'Are you stopping here? Innit lovely! I told you we should have stayed at this hotel, Derek. What's it like inside?'

Now I could have gone back and answered the first question, but this woman was obviously hungry for information, so I went straight on to the second.

'Well, the foyer's all pink and there's pot plants and big armchairs.'

'Oh, that's lovely. I wonder if we can change from ours, Derek. It can't be that much more. I'm Babs. That's my husband, Derek,' she said nodding towards the middle-aged man sitting up front with the driver.

Babs was in her fifties. She had jet-black hair backcombed high upon her head, bright blue eye-shadow, and false eyelashes that curled well into next week. Her skimpy tie-up blouse showed off her more-than-ample bosom, and her shorts revealed the beginnings of a tan. I wondered if she realized she was on a trip to a Muslim country.

'Have you found them bus tickets yet?' she called to Derek.

He replied in a stream of consciousness. 'I've got 'em here. They're in me pocket. I'm sitting on them. I'll find 'em when I get there. He's got us name down anyway. It don't matter.'

'Yes, that's fine,' said the driver.

Babs tutted.

The younger couple sitting at the back and I introduced ourselves. 'I'm Gill, this is my husband, Ian,' said the woman, who looked exceptionally tall and quite uncomfortable in the minibus.

'Tomorrow, will you find out how much extra that hotel is?' Babs called out.

'Yeah, all right,' replied Derek.

'He won't,' Babs declared to the rest of the bus.

A few moments later we stopped. A couple in their early forties got on with a girl aged about thirteen. Babs made a grab for the girl's arm to steady her way along to a seat. The girl shyly turned her head.

'Say thank you, Sarah,' said the woman quietly.

'That's everyone then,' said the guide.

No Mr Right on this trip then, I thought.

So for one reason or another, we all settled into a mood of reserve until we finished our short journey to the airport.

'I'll give the group ticket to you, Derek, all right?' – what a brilliant choice, I thought, giving it to a man who has lost one lot already. – 'And I'll see you back here at nine o'clock tonight,' continued the driver.

At Tangiers Airport we made our way towards a guide waving the logo we recognized.

'More people?' he asked.

'A couple more.'

Eventually we saw Derek and Babs making their way through customs.

'Who am I meant to give this bloody thing to then?' shouted Derek, trying to force the docket on to anyone in uniform.

The guide took it out of his hand.

'More people?' he asked again.

'No, that's it.'

He looked up angrily.

'Only eight people?'

'Yes.'

'OK, change your money here and then come outside,' he said abruptly.

Outside we found the guide sitting on the steps of a 52-seater coach. Yes, maybe he was expecting more people. He was in heated discussion with the driver and there was much contemptuous flicking of the docket. The driver started up the coach and we set off towards Tangiers.

'Shall we have a singsong?' asked the guide, launching into a chorus of 'Que Sera Sera'.

Nobody joined in.

'OK, we just drive,' he declared sulkily.

Three or four miles later the coach stopped and, from behind some bushes, a man stepped out on to the road. Coloured plastic necklaces dangled from each arm and he held a pile of sun-hats in each hand, with even more balanced on his head. The coach doors opened, he got on, walked up the coach, then back down the aisle, and got off again without making a sound or a sale. We continued on our journey.

'They do that everywhere,' Derek shouted to the rest of the coach. 'You want to watch out, else you can end up buying some right rubbish.'

A few more minutes up the road and we stopped again. In a clearing, four men stood with two camels.

'You want a camel ride?' asked the driver. Everyone looked at each other in wary anticipation and got off the coach.

'Do you want to have a go?' Babs asked the girl.

She nodded, so a man lifted her on. The rest of us followed in a whirlwind of dust; kneeling, spitting camels; sticks waving; men shouting; and of money changing hands. Within two minutes both men and camels had disappeared, and we had banded together for comfort. For reasons financial, humanitarian and veterinary it had not been an enjoyable experience, and we trooped sadly and guiltily back on to the coach.

'You like the camel ride?' the guide asked.

As we entered the outskirts of the city, our guide took pride in pointing out rich people's homes to us. Finally, the coach stopped in the bustling heart of Tangiers, and a Moroccan in traditional flowing white robes walked to the door of the coach. His welcoming smile began to waver as no more than eight passengers stepped out, and he climbed on to the coach to look inside for the rest of the party. He said something to the guide and the driver, and an argument broke out between the three men.

He got back off the coach and stood in front of us. 'My name is Abdul. I will take you to the casbah. Follow me close. Do not buy anything on the way. I will take you to the best shops, best price.' He strode off towards the walls of the market.

'See, I told you,' said Derek, 'you have to know what

you're doing in a place like this. You could end up buying some right crap.'

We set off at a sprinter's pace, missing the delights of the walled maze of shops and doorways, in a desperate bid to keep up with Abdul, who was by now disappearing into the distance like the dot at the end of a night's television viewing. Within seconds street sellers appeared, rushing alongside us, shouting at us to stop, like would-be stowaways trying to board a runaway train. We tried to keep track of our guide through the forest of bangles, baskets, sandals and brass ornaments swinging in front of our faces. Round the next corner – and there stood Abdul, as solid as a marble statue. Startled, we all fell into the person in front.

'This is the oldest house in the casbah,' said Abdul. We turned to look, grateful for a chance to catch our breath, but Abdul had already sprinted five yards ahead.

'Where's Derek?' shouted Babs breathlessly.

I turned round and saw Derek's beige trouser legs, an armoured brass chest of bowls, jugs and candlesticks, and a four-headed monster made up of three plastic camel faces and Derek's quiff.

'What did they stop here for?' he asked.

'The oldest house in the casbah,' I recited.

Derek strained to turn his head. A band of merchants had stopped with him, still thrusting trinkets into what was once the face of a grown man. I bought a wicker basket from one, and helped Derek unload his treasure into it.

'How much did you pay for that?' he asked.

'I don't know, about a pound.'

'Bloody hell, that's just his starting price!'

Babs reappeared. 'Come on, he's got a snake up here!'

Past the man with the snake and the camera, hurtling through, our entourage in full pursuit, we came to another abrupt halt as Abdul appeared, standing in a doorway. 'You come into good shop,' he said. He held out his arm and directed us into the cool and calm of a warehouse. The street sellers tried to follow, but a burly man blocked their way and we fled into sanctuary. Once inside, sipping the sickly drink we had been given, we were treated to a seemingly endless display of 'very beautiful' carpets. One by one we were taken aside and asked to consider how distraught our husbands, brothers, mothers and fathers might be, should we not bring home a hand-woven rug. Eventually Ian cracked and, by buying the smallest rug in the shop, led us all to our liberation.

'Is that all?' asked Abdul, slightly grieved. 'OK, we will have lunch now. I will take you to beautiful restaurant.'

We walked outside to where our old friends were faithfully waiting with their wares. A man standing in a doorway held up some mosque-window-shaped mirrors. Some were fake gold and some were three-coloured fake bronze, silver and gold. I quite liked them. To the trained eye, a flicker of interest could be picked up in an instant.

'You like this? One-colour, three-colour. You like?'

I pointed to a three-colour mirror. 'This one?'

'Fifty dirhams.'

'No, twenty,' I objected.

'No, one-colour twenty, three-colour fifty.'

'No, three-colour twenty,' I haggled.

'No, three-colour fifty.'

'No, no, no.'

We arrived at the restaurant, where his attempt to follow me inside was thwarted by the doorman.

'OK, twenty, twenty!' he yelled, and I gave him the twenty-dirham note and took the three-colour mirror out of his hand.

The owner of the restaurant led us up a tiled spiral staircase to a large table reserved for about forty people. We all turned to each other and smirked, waiting for yet another argument to break out. Abdul went off into the kitchen.

'Derek's been all round the world, you know,' Babs told us proudly, as the waiter brought some dishes of spiced meatballs.

'I was in the merchant navy,' said Derek.

'Have you been to Tangiers before?' I asked.

'No. I've been to Egypt, though – it's pretty much the same thing. I usually just make for the nearest bar.'

Abdul emerged from the kitchen after we'd eaten and announced there was somewhere else he wanted to take us. Walking down the staircase, I noticed a familiar face waiting in the doorway.

'One-colour twenty, three-colour fifty,' he continued, as if there had been no break in our bargaining.

'I've *got* a mirror!' I protested, holding it up.

He grabbed it. 'Three-colour! No twenty, one-colour twenty.' He held a gold mirror out to me. 'No, please, you take one-colour.'

I liked my mirror. I hesitated.

'Please,' he said, 'I have babies!'

'OK,' I said. I let go of the three-colour mirror and took the horrible gold one.

'OK,' he confirmed, and ran off to make up for lost time.

Derek arrived at the bottom of the stairs. 'Did you buy another one?' he asked.

'No, he wanted it back, he gave me a cheaper one.'

'Bloody crooks, aren't they?' he laughed.

Abdul was now walking at a slightly slower pace than before, and we managed to follow him out of the casbah without too much effort. Presently he stopped outside a glass-fronted doorway and directed us inside. 'Perhaps you will like these carpets better,' he ventured.

'Oh no, not more carpets!' we protested.

Abdul stared at us. 'I leave you now,' he retorted angrily, 'I have a headache,' and he walked off.

'Abdul,' we called, 'where's the coach?'

'It will come back!' he shouted.

'Where?'

Abdul pointed vaguely towards a side-street, where we could just spot a neon hotel sign.

'When?'

But Abdul had disappeared into the throng.

'Right, that's that then,' said Derek eventually. 'I think we should go up there and get a drink.'

Although he'd started off leading us up the hill, somehow Derek still managed to get left behind. When he eventually walked into the foyer, with his wicker basket, he had a two-foot-high black plaster elephant, covered in coloured sequins, peeking out from under his arm.

'What have you got there?' asked Babs.

'It's an elephant,' he said, placing it proudly on the table in front of us. 'Look at that, eh.'

We looked at it.

'I thought you told us not to buy a load of crap, Derek,' I said.

'That's not crap!' he proclaimed. 'That'd cost fifty quid if you bought it at home!'

'But you *wouldn't* buy it at home,' declared Babs.

'No, I know I wouldn't – I'm on my bloody holiday!'

Having all agreed to meet up again at that hotel in a couple of hours, some of us headed back down to the main street, where Ian stopped outside a shop selling ornamental swords.

'He collects knives and daggers,' Gill told us as he went in. She had collar-length light brown hair, wore glasses, and was almost five inches taller than Ian, who had a baby face and tattoos down each arm.

There were some Arab men sitting outside a café next door, and one started drawing the other's attention to Sarah.

'Very pretty. Is she married?'

Sarah giggled.

'Let's see how Ian's getting on, shall we?' said her father, guiding Sarah forcibly into the shop. The rest of us followed.

Inside, Ian was inspecting a sword that was nearly the same size as himself.

'Look at this one, feel that, it's really sharp!' he said, running his fingers along the edge of the blade.

Gill told him he'd never get it through customs.

'I might,' he said, 'it's only an ornament.'

'I don't care!' shrieked Gill. 'I'm not having it in the house!'

Ian hastily leant it back against the wall and began looking through a display of much smaller knives. I started to harbour suspicions about why he collected them in the first place.

'Oh come on, we don't want to be in here all day!' said Gill impatiently.

Sarah had wandered back to the doorway to see her admirers who were still outside. We all started to make our way out of the shop.

'I can walk on my own,' Sarah declared, brushing off her father's arm. Confidently she strode off down a side-road towards the sea, her anxious parents following on behind.

Ian, Gill and I continued along the main street. Gill stopped to look into a shop window at some sequined ornaments and kaftans. She pointed at a horribly double-jointed mannequin wearing a blue sparkly monstrosity. 'I like that,' she said. 'Will you buy me it, Ian?'

Ian looked a little confused, but agreed, and walked into the shop.

'Don't you want to try it on?' I asked.

'No, I don't like it. Do you? I just wanted to show you that he does anything I say.'

We saw the dress being taken off the model in the window. She'd even got him to do a runner from the honeymoon hotel in Cambridge five days ago, she told me.

'Oh, I didn't know you were on your honeymoon,' I said, surprised. Not wanting to be a gooseberry, I offered to wander off.

'No, it's nothing like that,' she said. 'I was nearly thirty and getting a bit des–'

Ian came out of the shop holding a brown paper bag. Gill took out the dress, said she didn't like it, and asked Ian to take it back. He went back into the shop.

'See what I mean?' she sighed.

We watched the kaftan being put back over the figure's head. Ian reappeared looking very pleased with himself.

'I couldn't get my money back so I got this knife instead,' he said.

Gill glowered.

Nearly three hours later, back at the hotel, it was obvious that Babs and Derek hadn't left the bar at all. A coach bearing the familiar logo pulled up outside and the driver came in. 'Where is your guide?' he asked.

'He had a headache and left us in the casbah!' Derek bellowed.

'Left us in the bloody lurch, more like!' screeched his wife.

On the way to the airport we saw a man standing by the side of the road.

'Stop!' Babs shouted, reeling to the front of the coach. 'He's that bloke with the beads. I haven't bought anything yet!' The driver stopped and opened the door. ' 'Ere y'are, come on love,' she said, flashing all the notes and loose change she had at him. He stepped on to the bus and, like some bizarre fairground hoopla, tried to get as many necklaces over Babs' beehive as he could, as she carefully arranged them around her cleavage. 'Give us one of them an' all,' she demanded, and plonked a pink straw sun-hat on top of her head.

His complete stock sold, we waved to a very happy bead man as we headed off into the sunset to the strains of 'Que Sera Sera'.

39. *Holly*

Captain's log: A Tuesday in July 1989. My agent rang.

'They want you to audition for *Red Dwarf*,' she told me. 'For the part of Holly.'

Norman was not doing the new series for some reason, and they were looking for a new Holly. The modest offices of Noel Gay TV were just off the Charing Cross Road, in 'Tin-Pan Alley', a road so nick-named because of its abundance of music shops. My appointment was for eleven-thirty, but because of my own brand of timing I had purposely written the time down in my diary as eleven, and my watch was, as usual, ten minutes fast.

'Yes, Hattie, I've got you down here,' said the reception-ist. 'You're a little bit early, and I'm afraid they're running a little bit late.' I wondered quite where that took us in the general time–space continuum. I looked at her upside-down list and read a few names I hadn't heard of before. They must be proper actors and actresses, I thought, slightly disheartened. 'They'll be about half an hour,' she continued, and I felt obliged to stop reading the list and look back at her face.

'That's all right.' I turned and looked out of the door at the sunny, bustling street. 'I'll go and get a drink and come back later,' I said, as I made my way out to a café and a cappuccino.

I returned about twenty minutes later.

'They're waiting to see you. Go straight down the stairs.'

That's all I need, I thought. Now I'm late. I walked down the narrow carpeted staircase and into a meeting room, and met Doug, Rob and Ed again.

'I was early, so I went and got a drink,' I explained.

'Hey, our kind of gal!' said Rob, obviously mistaking the cappuccino I'd had for eight pints of heavy.

We all had a chat, and I tried to read the rest of the upside-down list. Yes, one name I recognized, and, as I suspected, she was a proper actress.

Ed gave me a page of *Red Dwarf* script.

'If you could just read this,' he said.

I read it and laughed.

'Out loud,' he smiled.

'Oh, right!' I said.

'And see if it makes us laugh,' said Doug, 'because we've read it before.'

'Is this earth?'

'Yes.'

'What time period?'

'Lunch-time, maybe half one.'

We chatted some more, and I left. God, I thought, I hope I didn't mess that up. They *had* laughed when I read it, I'm sure they had.

Three days later, my agent rang.

'They want you to be Holly.'

I deafened her with one high-pitched excited squeal.

I put down the phone, thumped out a drum roll on the arm of the settee, and disappeared into a cloud of dust. One of these flatmates of mine really must give the house a good hoovering some time, I thought.

Immediately events moved magically fast. First, I had to be checked over by a showbiz doctor. Not one in a pink sparkly suit and an electric light-bulb bow-tie, but one who examines the actors in a television series to make sure they won't drop dead during filming. This is not so much motivated by the milk of human kindness as by the financial and administrative considerations of recasting and filming the scenes again.

A few days later I met up again with Craig, Danny and Chris to read through the scripts in Acton. Robert Llewellyn had also joined the regular cast, and he was immediately whisked away to another room with Rob and Doug, to work out how to walk and talk as a robot. I knew Robert also from the comedy circuit – he was especially memorable for doing his act in tight-fitting black Lycra cycling shorts.

The first episode to be filmed for series III was called 'Marooned'. This was to be rehearsed by the cast from the last week of August. Because Robert and I had been cast only fairly recently for the series, we both already had three weeks of shows booked at the Edinburgh Festival, lasting until Saturday 2 September. The producers had agreed we could miss the week's rehearsals, but we both had to be back for the technical run-through in London at ten o'clock on the Sunday morning. They arranged for a taxi to take me to Edinburgh Airport, where I'd pick up my tickets, catch the seven o'clock plane to Heathrow, and be whisked off in another taxi straight to the Acton rehearsal rooms.

Robert was doing a play in the Assembly Rooms in the late afternoon on Saturday, and I was doing a show with comic and poet Henry Normal in the same room at midnight. From the end of Robert's show to the beginning of ours, there were probably four or five other acts that would take place in this particular room. By the time our show started, it was already the Sunday morning.

The flat where Henry and I were staying was very close to the performers' last-night party. I worked out that, even if I went to bed straight after the show, I'd get about four hours' sleep at the most, so it seemed a better idea to stay awake. My mind and body had gone into a kind of night-shift mode anyway. I'd go to the party, do a bit of early-morning packing, have a bath, and then wait for the taxi.

I arrived back at the flat at three-thirty in the morning, opened my bag, looked in, closed it, and opened it again. No, my keys were definitely not in there. I sighed, cursed, then walked back to the party to find Henry. I wandered around the bar and dance floor, saying hallo to people who ten minutes before I'd said goodbye to, asking if they'd seen him. Nobody knew where he'd gone, but he'd last been seen leaving. So I went back to the flat. There were no lights on and no one answered the door. I went back to the party, and back to the flat, and back to the party for the next couple of hours, like an engine shunting up and down on a single-track branch line.

Eventually, feet throbbing, I slumped down on the freezing cold concrete steps outside the flat. I was marooned. At six o'clock, just as it was getting light, a taxi arrived to take me to the airport.

'Been waiting long?' the driver asked.

'All night.'

'Any luggage?'

'Yes, but I can't get to it.'

I arrived on time at the tech-run and, with a deep breath, walked into the rehearsal room. It was a casual kind of day, everyone was wearing jeans or track suits. I arrived that Sunday morning wearing high-heeled shoes, laddered tights, the remains of last night's make-up, and a blue frilly fifties cocktail dress. 'I thought I'd make a bit of an effort,' I said, 'since it's the first show.' I could see in their faces that, for a moment there, they really believed me.

In every spare moment of this rehearsal I was phoning the flat in Edinburgh, and I eventually got hold of Henry. I had to describe all my possessions over the phone so he could do my packing. It was like a cross between some bizarre memory test and virtual reality without the screen.

'Where are you now?'

'I'm by the dressing-table.'

'The make-up and bottles on the right-hand side, they're

mine, the rest of the stuff is the landlady's. Now, go over to the window-sill . . .'

Luckily Henry lived in Manchester, where we were filming, so he met me that Sunday night with my luggage. I opened the suitcase and looked inside. It was amazing – some of the things in it even belonged to me.

40. *Looking for Adventure*

Twice now, I've gone on one of those holidays that offer adventure trips across little-known tracks in the remotest of places. Of course, it is obvious that if a tour company goes there and has a glossy brochure on every travel agent's shelf, then it is not going to be a remote little track known only to your nomadic yak herdsman. You can take it for granted that if you can get there, so can a million other tourists, and probably on the same day.

My combined trip to Malaysia, Thailand and Singapore lasted nearly three weeks, if you count getting to the airport. It's important to remember that if you go on one of these trips without your own playmate, then you are going to be sharing a room with a total stranger. This list is compiled by the holiday company, and your room-mate has been decided by them before you've had a chance to get to know anyone. Therefore, you have to make snap judgements. If there is someone you have liked or disliked on sight, it is important to grab the guide before this list has been called out on the first night. Otherwise it takes a United Nations directive to get it changed afterwards.

To keep the cost down, though you wouldn't think it, the flights on these adventure holidays take the long and dangerous way round, usually via the Middle East. Now you may think this should depend on where you're going, but I don't think it does. I think even the flight to Scotland on one of these trips would involve five stops – three of which would be a mile apart in various countries in the Middle East. However, if you've missed the distinctive labels on other people's luggage at the check-in, this change of planes can be advantageous. By using your powers of deduction, and watching who, from the last flight, is also on the next one, you can work out who is likely to be in your adventure group before you reach the company logo on a stick at the final destination airport.

Standing in the check-in queue in front of me at Heathrow was a short woman dressed frumpier than her years, with her light brown hair in the style of a middle-aged woman's perm. Next to her was an older woman, dressed younger than her age. I noticed the younger one had the same luggage tag as I did, and at the same time the older woman turned round and noticed this too.

'Are you going to Malaysia?' she asked.

'Yes, I am,' I said.

'Have you been abroad before?'

'Yes, not on one of these adventure trips, but I have been abroad before.'

'Oh good,' she said, 'would you mind looking after my daughter, because she hasn't?' I looked at the daughter, who was probably in her thirties. 'Could you sit next to her on the plane?' continued the mother.

'That's the easy part, sitting on the plane,' I said, 'you can't go wrong then.'

We got closer to the check-in, and I started to hang back a little. I was trying to work out what the problem was, as the daughter seemed to have all her faculties, apart from her dress sense. I could sit next to her, I suppose.

'My mum does fuss!' she told me in an irritatingly whining voice.

No, I'm sorry, I thought, eighteen hours, I'd go mad.

The mother got to the check-in, grabbed my case along with her daughter's, and said, 'Can you put these two together?'

No, this was not a way to start a holiday I'd paid so much for, by doing something I really didn't want to do.

'Oh my God!' I shrieked. 'I've left another bag by the phone box. I'd better go and get it.'

The check-in woman picked up the security phone. 'It's probably been taken away by now,' she told me sternly.

'No, it's all right, it's just over there. I can see it.'

The woman and daughter stepped to one side.

'We'll wait here for you,' they said.

'No, don't do that, it's all right, don't worry.'

'We'll hold your case till you come back,' they went on.

'No, I'd better take it with me!' I shrieked. 'Won't be a minute, carry on!' and, rapidly turning into Basil Fawlty, I grabbed the trolley and ran off towards a wall of phones. I quickly sneaked into a concourse shop, where I stayed for a good fifteen minutes, looking at ties. Finally I thought it was safe to come out. I edged my way back to the check-in desks, to find the pair of them still standing there, waiting. They waved, and I felt myself being drawn to my doom.

'Did you find your bag?' they asked.

'No,' I had to say, because I obviously didn't have another bag with me. The check-in woman picked up the phone again. 'No, I remember now. I phoned home and I've left it by the front door. It's at home!' I said. 'Never mind. Nothing in it.' I laughed nervously.

'I've managed to save you two seats together,' said the check-in woman proudly.

'Where are they?' I asked. 'I'd like to sit by the window.'

'I've put your friend in the window seat.'

'That's fine,' I said. 'I'll sit by another window.'

My 'friend' didn't mind not sitting by the window.

'No! you sit there,' I said, 'you'll love it.' My voice was starting to get louder. Was I really going to have to spell it out? 'I'll sit somewhere else,' I said, quietly and firmly.

'I can put you in the window seat behind,' said the check-in woman helpfully.

'That would be fine.'

We checked in, the mother sent her daughter off with a tearful farewell, and we wandered together through the security and passport control. I told her the gist of duty-free, but there wasn't a lot of time left for that now.

We got on the plane and found there was an empty seat next to each of us. That's good, I told her, we can both get a bit of sleep. I spoke rather too soon in her case, as the last passenger came on board and sat next to her.

A few minutes after take-off, when the seat-belt light

went out, she stood up and started waving her arm. A hostess was on the spot in seconds. She leant across and I heard her whisper, 'Yes, that's fine.' The man next to her stood up and my 'friend' clambered out, then clambered into my row. I hastily moved my clutter before she sat on it.

'There was an Arab next to me!' she whispered in alarm.

The main reason I had chosen this trip above all the other countless possibilities was the four nights we would be spending in a lodge in the jungle. It was well over ten years since I'd visited the nursery or a jungle, and I was getting kind of homesick. One of these nights was to be spent in a hut next to a waterhole, watching the animals as they came down to drink. I had bought a good-quality tape recorder especially to capture the night sounds of the birds and any animals we might encounter.

There were fifteen of us in the group, and when we reached this part of the trip, the guide told us there was only room for eight people in the hut, so half of us would spend all four nights in the lodge.

'So we'll draw lots,' she said. 'If you get a cross on your piece of paper, you stay in the hut.'

'Why don't we see how many people definitely want to stay in the hut,' I suggested, 'then work it out from there?'

'No, it's fairer if we draw lots,' she insisted.

'No it isn't,' I said. 'Some people might not want to stay in the jungle hut.'

This started everybody off. Some didn't know there was a jungle hut on offer, and some didn't care either way.

Red Dwarf – Holly and Hilly

Chris Barrie and Robert Llewellyn relaxing

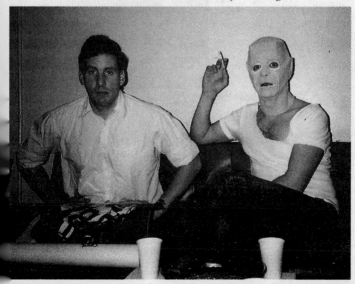

(*Above*) Danny John-Jules –
I don't know what he's
talking about

(*Right*) Craig Charles – holy
flying dreadlocks

(*Below left*) Rob Grant and
Doug Naylor getting fired up

Red Dwarf – on location with Elvis

Meeting the Holly Man in Chicago

Mellie – sweet as a cherry

In 'Quarantine' at Dimension Jump '96

She started to give out folded-up pieces of paper. I started to rant.

'We left the jungle – we've been through millions of years of evolution, and we're deciding by a mark on a bit of paper. We might as well have bloody stayed there,' I argued.

'Well, it's fairest,' she said.

'Well I'm going anyway,' I said. 'It's the only reason I came on this bloody trip.'

I unfolded my piece of paper. It was blank. The hotel lodge for me then, in theory. An American woman next to me started to open up her piece of paper with her well-manicured coral-pink nails, and tossed back her long blonde wavy hair.

'I've got a cross on mine. What does that mean?'

I snatched it out of her hand. 'It means you're in the hotel,' I said.

'Oh thank God!' she squealed.

We saw a tapir that night. Granted most people couldn't pick a tapir out in a police line-up, but I'd seen it, and recorded it grunting over the dawn chorus, and that's what mattered.

I know they are making a medicinal comeback but, nevertheless, the first mention in the guidebook of the word 'leeches' spurred me on to develop my own personal style of jungle wear, designed so that they couldn't get anywhere near me. This ensemble has a kind of Victorian-English-gentlewoman-meets-American-footballer look to it, and consists of ankle boots, long socks over the top of long harem-style trousers, a long-sleeved shirt, a cotton hat worn over a chiffon scarf draped around the head and neck, and long cotton gloves. This little outfit, all in matching white, is, although I say so myself, rather fetching. Some people, usually wearing shorts and boob tube, have been known to call it 'ridiculous', before they have spent many a long hysterical hour trying to pick off the blood-sucking little parasites. I would quite happily have included a photo of me in this complete outfit but, unfortunately, in the jungle it is impossible to stand far enough away from a person to take a full-length photo without a tree getting in the way.

In Penang, there were monkeys that lived in the botanical gardens. Not in cages, but just wandering around, since it had been their home even before an entrance fee had come into existence. As a group, we walked round and were then supposed to head back to the hotel for no particular reason. At the gate I spotted a man selling big bags of small bananas, and I told the guide that I'd like to stay longer and make my own way back. I bought a bag of bananas and went back to feed the monkeys. Something in my memory should have put two and two together, but unfortunately it didn't.

Once the monkeys saw I had food they came wandering up to me. It was thirsty work and I got a can of drink out of my bag. I threw them the bananas one by one, and they sat down, peeled them and ate them. I wondered if they learnt to peel bananas from us, or if we learnt it from them. The largest monkey of the group appeared out of the bushes to claim his rightful share just as I had one banana left. I threw it to him. He caught it, and didn't peel and eat it, but put it down by his side. He obviously wanted to save it for later. He sat on the ground in front of me, fixing me with a determined stare. I know he's going to jump at me, I thought, I can see it in his eyes. I realized he had recognized my can of Coke as a brand he liked, and as I glanced towards it, he leapt up and grabbed it out of my hand. He sat on the path, swigging it down contentedly. I knew there wasn't that much drink left, and it wasn't chilled, so calmly and briskly I walked towards the middle of a crowd of people.

41. *Thailand*

A friend's cousin had been killed on a motor-bike by a hit-and-run driver in Thailand. His mother asked me, if I found myself on that island and in the area, could I take a photo of his grave. I felt guilty somehow to be going to a place on holiday, when she had a much more compelling reason to go. She gave me the name of a Thai girl he'd been living with, and the address, such as it was, of the bar where she worked.

As we made our way on to various ferry boats I asked our Thai guide if we would be heading anywhere near this island. He told me that we would be staying there only for a night and a day, but not to worry, there was plenty of time for sunbathing in the next place. I explained to him that sunbathing wasn't the reason I was asking.

We arrived on the island in the early evening, and I asked him again about the bar. He asked around and was told it was a couple of miles out of the main town. He shrugged his shoulders, and told me that it would soon be getting dark.

'I'll get a taxi,' I said.

He didn't seem to think this was a very good idea. He took my arm and gently sat me down at a table in the hotel gardens.

'I don't really know how to say this,' he started in a quiet voice, 'but you must understand that Thai girls are very poor, and the girls that work in bars may have many boyfriends. Perhaps she doesn't remember him.'

His reluctance hadn't been indifference, he had wanted to spare my feelings.

'Thank you,' I said. I had to admit that these thoughts had crossed my own mind. 'I understand what you're saying. His mother asked me to find her, and if the girl doesn't remember him, I'll have to say we didn't get to the island.'

He suddenly clasped my hand across the table, and stood up. 'I have a friend with a motor-bike, I will take you there.'

It was not a tarmac road, and there were no lights, apart from the glimmer of a few houses on the way, and I don't really think he was used to driving a motor-bike. We drove a couple of miles out, and stopped at the first bar. We were looking for the Umbrella Bar. There was nothing here with that name. We set off again into total darkness for a couple of miles. He turned and called out to me, 'I don't think it's this far.' A truck with no lights came hurtling along the road and passed us. 'We'd better go back,' he said, slightly panicked, and turned the bike round. He drove a little way, then pulled in again at the bar we'd seen before. STAR BAR shone the bright blue neon sign. 'Maybe they know where it is.'

We walked in and immediately saw a hundred coloured-paper umbrellas hanging from the ceiling.

'I think this is it!' I said.

As I looked around at the two or three customers, my eyes were drawn to a corner of the bar. I gasped, and instinctively my hands rose up to my face. A gleaming black-and-chrome motor-bike leant against the wall; immaculate, yet crushed. I walked towards the broken frame. It was adorned with fresh flowers that trailed on to a table where some keepsakes were laid out and where a scented candle burned brightly. Above this shrine hung a photo of a young man I recognized. He certainly hadn't been forgotten.

'I don't believe this,' I whispered, and turned to the guide, now standing by my side and wiping his eyes.

A girl came out to serve us.

'Hallo,' said the guide, 'we are looking for . . .'

I gave her name.

A small, slim, beautiful Thai girl walked out from the back room. She looked at us and smiled.

'Hallo,' I said. 'Steven's mother asked me to come and see how you are.'

We hugged and stood in tears in the middle of the bar.

The next day she took me to the grave. The Buddhist cemetery was a calm, serene place, the atmosphere thick with the fragrance of incense, and somehow very much alive. A monk in flowing orange robes was going about his daily tasks; fetching buckets of water and heating them over burning sticks. I took the photo for his mother, as dogs played around the paths and cats lay sleeping on the steps of the temple.

42. *Singapore Feet*

My feet were the worst they'd ever been. I could have sworn they started to swell up the moment I went through passport control at Heathrow. By the time we arrived in Bangkok they were little pink rugby balls. After we had travelled through Thailand, Malaysia, the rainforest, and arrived in Singapore, they were red rubber washing-up gloves that had been blown up with a bicycle-pump. The only shoes I could wear were giant-sized flip-flops. The size, shape and colour of my feet, plus the insect bites, would have combined to make an interesting conversation point if only people had had the stomach to mention them.

Singapore is a clean, clinical city-state, whose rulers have bulldozed down the back alleys and purged the porn and sleaze for which it was once famous in previous generations. It now consists almost entirely of identical inter-connecting shopping centres selling cameras, computers, and clothes that are two sizes too small. The British have left traces of their civilization in the guise of English cream teas, so one Sunday afternoon, dressed in a long flowing cotton dress, I went into an old colonial hotel to sample the delights.

I entered through the revolving doors into the grand

foyer, and walked flip-flop flip-flop towards the restaurant, where I waited to be seated.

'Good afternoon, madam, will you be taking tea alone this afternoon?' asked a Chinese man in a white uniform trimmed with gold braid.

'Yes please.'

He bowed a low bow and in doing so, caught his first glimpse of the two wobbly stacks of blancmange at the ends of my legs.

'I'm very sorry, madam, we cannot allow people into the restaurant who are wearing sandals,' he said politely. To describe the planks I was wearing as sandals was well beyond any duty of politeness. Curiously, and perhaps owing to the prevailing colonial atmosphere, I found myself turning into Celia Johnson.

'I'm very sorry,' I trilled sweetly, 'my feet have swollen in the heat. I'm afraid I can only wear sandals.'

'One moment, please,' he said, and went off. He reappeared with another Chinese waiter, who was decorated with slightly more gold braid.

'Good afternoon, madam,' he bowed, taking in a good look at my feet. 'I'm sorry, we cannot allow people to wear sandals in the restaurant.'

'Oh dear, I'm very sorry,' I replied, 'my feet have swollen in the heat and I cannot wear any other shoes.'

'One moment, I will talk to the manager.'

Leaving the first waiter to stand guard, he went off and returned with a Chinese man ranked so highly in the chain of command that he didn't need to wear a uniform.

'Good afternoon, madam.' He bowed and stared. 'I'm

very sorry, we do not allow people into the restaurant who are wearing sandals,' he said politely but firmly.

'Yes, I'm very sorry,' I persisted sweetly, never forgetting for one instant that a cream tea was at stake here. 'The heat makes my feet swell, and I can only wear sandals.'

He stepped back and called his colleagues over. A huddled whispered discussion ensued. The first waiter came back over to me.

'Madam, we let you into the restaurant, but may we seat you in a corner, so your feet do not upset our other patrons? Do you agree?'

'Yes, that's fine,' I said, delighted.

'And also,' he continued, 'you do not go to the table, we will bring the food to you.'

'Yes, yes,' I agreed.

We had arrived at a consensus and everyone was happy. The manager, the waiter with an excess of braid, and the minion waiter, all walked alongside me, shielding the people who were eating from the sight of my feet. In the centre of the room was a huge table layered like a wedding cake and decorated with sandwiches and cream fancies of every description. People stood around armed with tongs and side-plates. We walked quickly past. I was shown to a table and chair close to the kitchen door. I sat down and in an instant was surrounded by a heavy carved wooden screen. More confession than confection.

A waiter I hadn't seen before appeared first with my pot of tea, followed in time by a procession of waiters bringing huge plates of crustless sandwiches, scones, cream and jam, and cream cakes. The waiters giggled as they brought each new course, and took away the empty plates. I realized in retrospect that I was probably meant to select from these plates, not eat the whole lot. There I was in my own private paradise, disturbed only by the approach of more food, and the intermittent sight of heads that would suddenly appear round the screen to look at me, and report back to their fellow diners.

43. Mum

Mum had not felt at all well at the hotel in Torquay and had wanted to go home. So, battling illness and the Christmas train service, we eventually found our way back. The rounds of doctors, consultants and out-patient departments took up the first few months of 1990, and in May she was taken into hospital.

One day the nurse called me in.

'The consultant's coming round tomorrow, and he'll tell your mother about her cancer.'

'I don't think that's a very good idea,' I said. 'She really wouldn't want to know.'

'Well, in our experience,' said this not-yet-qualified nurse, 'we find it's best to tell people.'

'But in my experience of my mother,' I said, 'she wouldn't want to know.'

The nurse suggested that I could perhaps be there with Mum when the consultant told her.

I arrived at the hospital the next day, an hour early to make sure I didn't miss him.

'He's already been,' said the nurse.

'So, has he told her?'

'Yes.'

'How is she?' I asked.

'She seems to have taken it very well.'

I walked over to the bed. Mum looked happy enough.

'I'm going on a fortnight's holiday,' she laughed.

'What do you mean?'

She showed me a picture of a detached house in its own grounds. I looked at the brochure of a convalescent home.

'What did the consultant say?' I asked.

'A load of long words. I don't know what he was on about,' she replied.

One Sunday afternoon in May, I drove her out to the Essex countryside, to this convalescent home run by nuns. It felt odd. I wondered how she'd get on. Maybe this was how a mother felt leaving her child at school on the first day, I thought.

One evening, in the communal lounge, the other women introduced her to the game of I Spy. She felt she'd got the hang of it.

'I spy with my little eye, something beginning with . . .' her eyes searched around the room '. . . TV.'

The others looked a little confused.

'Is it the TV?' a woman asked, cautiously.

'Yes, that's right.'

Mum was still convinced she had been sent to a holiday camp, and she treated it as such. Maybe it was the nuns' black and white head-dresses that reminded her, but regularly, just before eleven o'clock in the morning, she would disappear off into the village. Eventually one of the patients asked her where she went.

'I go up to the pub and have a Guinness,' my mum told her.

'Can I come tomorrow?' asked the woman.

The nuns hadn't noticed my mum going missing for an hour, but gradually, under her influence, more and more women started to disappear at about this time. The nuns assumed their charges had gone off for long walks in the grounds, but wondered why they could never see them from the windows.

One lunch-time, they saw a dozen or so of their patients walk in through the front gate.

'Where have you all been?' the sister asked with concern, and in some panic.

The women hesitated.

'I always have a Guinness every day,' Mum explained simply.

The nuns had never had to deal with this sort of truancy before, but they came to the conclusion that if it made the women feel better, then they might as well let them go up the pub.

Her departure, two weeks later, coincided with this haven being closed down, owing to economic cuts. By June, Mum needed looking after full time, so I moved back home with her. Ron, the pub landlord, and his wife Joyce again lent us a single bed, and Mum slept downstairs in the front room. Friends, neighbours and relatives arrived in a steady stream, always offering to help in any way they could. I ran out of ideas of things for them to do. I'd say something vague like, 'I think the tea towels need folding up,' and immediately one of my aunts would be in the kitchen drawer sorting them out.

That year, Jack Dee and I were due to do three weeks at the Edinburgh Festival together. By August, Mum was very ill, and I knew I couldn't go. I arranged to see the promoter on a Sunday afternoon, a week before the festival started, to tell him. The publicity had all been done, the thousands of posters were printed and pasted up around the city, and he would have to find another act to put in his main show, but he really understood that there was no question about it.

One Friday evening in the middle of August, an aunt and a cousin came round. They saw Mum was sleeping, so they came into the back room and we had a cup of tea.

'Anything you need doing?' asked my aunt.

I was at a loss. 'The oven door doesn't shut properly.'

It hadn't shut properly for the last fifteen years, but I was getting desperate for plausible jobs. My cousin was out in the kitchen like a shot. He crouched down and started lifting the oven door up and down over the latch, then tried it again from a standing position. Maybe a bit of force was needed. Slam! Slam!

'I'll see if Mum's awake yet,' I said, and went into the front room.

I looked into her face.

Slam.

Breath.

Slam.

Breath.

I held her hand.

'Have you got a screwdriver?'

Breath.

Slam.

'Where do you keep your screwdrivers?'

Slam.

Breath.

'Is Lil awake yet?' my aunt shouted.

No.

Bye, Mum.

44. *It's a Laugh*

A lot of people say, 'Stand-up comedy must be the worst job in the world.' Someone once said to comic Mike Hayley, 'I couldn't get up there and do that.' That man was the pilot of the leading plane of the Red Arrows display team.

I've done gigs in small rooms above pubs, in 3,000-seater theatres, in fields, in tents, on a beach, on boats that don't go anywhere, on castle ramparts, in an asylum and in Glasgow's Barlinnie high-security prison. Sometimes the situation surrounding a gig proves to be more problematic than the gig itself.

Jack Dee and I did lots of gigs together during the winter of 1990/91. I was driving us to the West Midlands Arts Centre in Birmingham once. We had asked just about everyone for directions and nobody we asked had ever heard of the place.

'They'll know in here,' I said, and pulled into a police training college. The policeman on the desk had never heard of the place, and he called various people from up the corridor, and they didn't know either.

'Surely someone must know,' we said, but nobody did.

We walked back out of the building, unimpressed at the standard of teaching on the Giving Directions course. We hoped they were better at the Catching Dangerous Criminals option. We doubted it – not if they were hiding at the West Midlands Arts Centre. I reversed the car into the driveway next door to the college to turn round.

'Mind that post!' said Jack.

What, that post saying WEST MIDLANDS ARTS CENTRE?

I was coming back from a gig with a comic in his Mercedes. Despite the car being a bargain, he couldn't afford to tax or insure it, or, apparently, to put new bulbs in the back lights. On the motorway we were stopped by the police. He got out of the car straight away, and wandered over to the police car, to save them noticing the lack of tax disc.

'Where are you going?'

'London.'

'Where have you been?'

'Sheffield.'

The policeman started to walk round the car. He appeared in front of the windscreen. He's about to spot there's no tax, I thought. But no, just before he got to the gap where the tax should be, he walked back to the comic.

'Does your wife know about her?' he asked.

I arrived at St Helens by train, and tried to get a taxi from the station to the theatre.

'It'll cost you a pound. It's a waste of money, it's just down the road,' the taxi-driver said.

'I don't care, it's raining.'

'But I'm saving you money, don't you see.'

'I don't care,' I said, sounding like a rich London yuppie.

I walked along with my overnight case, getting soaked, swearing to myself about the stupid taxi-driver, and looking for this place just down the road that I couldn't miss. I stopped and asked an old man. 'Do you know where the Sentinel is please?'

He looked at me. 'Oh dear, love, no, it's not a Salvation Army hostel any more, they've made it into a theatre.'

I thought I'd just managed to get on the last train back to London moments before it pulled out of Portsmouth Harbour Station. However, I started to suspect something when a) I was the only one on it; b) we went through spinning wet brushes; and c) the lights went off. I pulled down the window and stuck my head out. I was at some kind of depot. There was no platform, and it was about a seven-foot drop to the ground, or whatever was there in the dark.

'Hallo!' I called. 'Hallo!'

The driver was walking along the track. 'How did you get on this train?' he asked.

'It was in the station.'

'I'll get someone to help you down.'

Another railway man appeared. 'Put your foot on here,' he said. He cupped his hands together.

'Isn't there a ladder?' I asked.

'Not really. Grab hold, you'll be all right.'

I darted back into the carriage, then handed him down my case. I stepped out of the train and, still clinging to the train door, put one foot on to his hands.

'Let go of the door!' he cried. 'I've got you.'

I let go of the door, my other knee landed on his shoulder and I clung on to his hair. He struggled to hold my weight. I started giggling. This was like something from a pornographic film of Laurel and Hardy meets the Kama Sutra. Somehow sliding on to his back, I managed to get my feet on the ground. I was still giggling.

'We'd better get you on to that London train,' he said, straight-faced.

We walked briskly along the track to an office, where he phoned the guard at the next station, who agreed to hold the London train while this man drove me there in his car. And all this for the price of a cheap-day return.

Three of us were doing a show at the Montreux Comedy Festival in Switzerland, and were to be met at the airport. We arrived, and there was no one holding up our names, or any other relevant words. We hung around a while, there were no announcements over the Tannoy. We searched again along the line where people holding cardboard signs were still waiting. Our last resort was the man we'd avoided when we arrived, the one holding up a huge cardboard banana. We looked at each other, the same thought in our minds. Would this be an example of the Swiss sense of humour? We nodded, and yes, this was indeed the man. It made me think that the only connection between Switzerland and comedy is timing.

I sometimes get recognized 'in the street', a loose term, because there have been many other places, including the Ladies toilet in Planet Hollywood. Sometimes it's for being me, and sometimes it's for being somebody else. Fairly recently I was with two other comics in an all-night pizza take-away in Oxford when a group of teenage lads came in. One looked at me, then looked again, then said, 'You're that girl off the telly, aren't you?' He pointed me out to his mates, 'Look, it's her off the telly.'

They all turned to look at me, and my two comedy chums were starting to get edgy, more for their own sakes than mine.

'It is you, isn't it?'

I smiled and shrugged.

'Wait till I tell my mum,' the first one continued, 'she loves *Heartbeat*.'

'It *is* you, isn't it?'

'Yes,' I lied. When it comes to spotting people off the telly, I suppose one celeb is pretty much like any other, I thought.

'I knew it was!' he shouted excitedly at the others.

His mates now also agreed that they recognized me. As we left, they followed me along on the pavement, shuffling on their knees, raising their arms and chanting, 'We are not worthy!'

I've also had to convince people I'm not Rodney's wife in *Only Fools and Horses*.

I've had to sign all manner of things: clothes, a car, beer bellies. After a stand-up gig in Hull a large student came up and quite politely asked if I'd sign his bum.

'My mates didn't think I'd ask you,' he said.

'Well, I'd better sign it in front of them on stage then,' I suggested, hoping this might put him off. Of course, it only encouraged him, and I had to buy a whole new set of felt-tips after that.

'Who writes your jokes?' someone asked me after a show.

'I do,' I said.

'Really!' he said, surprised, 'because I didn't think you really understood them.'

I had a coughing fit during a gig and, as it was near the end of my act anyway, I just croaked, 'Good night,' and left the stage, still coughing, with tears streaming down my face. Some people came up and congratulated me on. 'That ending was brilliant. How do you do that?'

Occasionally, something inexplicable will make an audience react as one hysterical mass.

One Saturday late-night show at Jongleurs Club, I was due on second after the interval, following an American doing an open spot. We'd met him for the first time in the dressing-room, and had marked him down as a bit of a weirdo. He was a laid-back Californian hippy, with long straggly hair, wearing dark red baggy cotton trousers and an embroidered waistcoat. He walked on stage with a bucket of washing-up liquid and a long broom handle with a large wire ring on the end. He put the bucket down, and drawled, 'Hi, I usually do children's parties.'

There were a few sniggers, because some people assumed he was going to be a comedy character. He dipped the wire ring into the bucket, and made a low swoop with the pole, over the heads of the audience. Bubbles trailed out across the room, and slop dripped over the heads of the people in the first few rows. The audience started to get a bit annoyed. He dipped the handle in again and created another stream of slop and bubbles. They got even more annoyed, and there were shouts for him to get off.

'No, no,' he protested, 'you'll like this next one.'

The audience calmed down a little. Maybe he was being a character after all, and this was to be the big punch-line, the hilarious grand finale. He put the broom handle in the bucket, lifted it up and swung it round over their heads, exactly as he had before. The audience now felt totally duped. They were annoyed out of all proportion to the crime. They got violently angry. In no time, a couple of hundred people were standing on chairs and tables shouting 'F★ck off!' – some with throbbing blue veins standing out on their necks. The management were signalling from the back for him to get off the stage, but he was still trying to win them over. 'Well, what about this one?' he continued, dipping the handle back in the bucket.

Bob Mills, the compère, walked on stage. 'Thank you, mate,' he said, forcibly helping him off. The Bubble Man tried to make his way out through baying, bulging angry red faces.

Bob tried to calm the audience down. 'Come on, what's the matter with you, he's only made a few bubbles. It's not like he's shagged your old woman.'

'I'd rather he had!' bellowed a purple-faced man, standing on his chair.

I'd have been laughing by now, if I wasn't about to go on next.

Bob was gradually calming them down to below boiling-point. 'You want to be standing up here!' he shouted, slipping and sliding all over the stage. 'I'm like bloody Torvill and Dean up here.'

The hippy was about to put this right. He walked back into the room and headed down to the front with a cloth and a bucket. At this second glimpse of him the audience resumed their screaming and yelling. He walked on to the stage, knelt down and started to wipe the floor.

'Come on, mate, leave it, all right?' pleaded Bob. 'Just piss off!'

The manager came in, grabbed the hippy and dragged him out.

In a moment of calm, Bob announced, 'Please welcome Hattie Hayridge.'

Not the words I was longing to hear.

Bob was one of the few people who could handle this situation, but the audience were now rabid. I made a few jokes about bubbles, a few other jokes, and lasted about five minutes before I got off. The act after me lasted about the same amount of time.

I walked out of the club. It was about one in the morning, but the sky was bright. Sometimes, I really do wonder about full moons . . .

45. *Red Dwarf*

'This is not a drill.'

This is Holly.

Between the second and third series, Holly the computer underwent a sex change, from male to female, from Norman Lovett to myself. The story-line was that the male Holly had fallen so much in love with his counterpart, Hilly, that he'd changed his face to hers. The 'senile bald old git' Holly was now younger, blonde and female. Apart from her appearance, Holly was somehow neuter but, in her own way, still the senile bald old git. The dry and deadpan style was very much like my own stand-up; physically, too, both parts were similar, the only movement being in my facial expressions. Technically, it would have been possible to record the Holly lines separately, then slot them into the show afterwards. Luckily, the producers had decided from the very beginning that Holly would be part of the same rehearsal and recording schedule as the rest of the cast.

The recording of a series of six episodes took six weeks for me, although the rest of the cast started filming on location two weeks earlier. For the third series, we still rehearsed at Acton, then recorded the show at the Manchester BBC studios. We made the journey in our own specially hired executive coach, complete with tables, little lamps, and our own hostess providing a continuous supply of teas, coffees and KitKats. The journey up, as we watched science fiction videos on the telly, was relatively sane, but coming back immediately after the recording, the atmosphere was electric.

Arthur Smith, who I knew from the comedy circuit, played and pretty much ad libbed the pub manager in the 'Backwards' episode of series III. In Edinburgh, Arthur represents the fun side of the festival as opposed to the commercial, and on one of the last nights he runs an alternative tour of the city. Starting at about three in the morning, a hundred or so drunken comics and curious insomniac members of the public follow Arthur round the deserted streets while being told a pack of lies. One year he discovered a huge pantechnicon trailer outside a concert hall. 'This is Edinburgh Cathedral,' he told us, and led us all in singing 'All Things Bright and Beautiful' while the removal men cursed and tried to push us out of the way with their Wagnerian scenery.

This was the year Lester Piggott was put in prison for tax fraud, and Arthur lied that he was being held in Edinburgh. On to the police station we went, chanting, 'Free Lester Piggott'. Very quickly, police in a dozen squad cars with flashing lights arrived in the hope of making a few arrests, and met with a mob of people bending at the knee, chanting, 'Hallo, hallo, hallo.' They moved us on.

Close to the police station was a tramp asleep on a bench. He'd taken off his shoes and left them neatly on the ground, as if he expected them to be cleaned by a bellboy during the night. 'Right, everybody put a pound in this bloke's shoes,' ordered Arthur. So we crept over and did just that, childishly excited at the prospect that this old man would wake up in the morning and think the tooth fairy had had a seizure.

At the end of the third series, the Manchester studios were closed for refurbishment, so the fourth and fifth series were rehearsed and filmed at Shepperton studios, in West London. This was where most of the James Bond films had been made, so I assumed it would be glamorous. I'd never visited film studios before, and I expected to see a vision reminiscent of Hollywood in its heyday. The truth is, it looked more like Lydd Airport during its construction phase. Most of the filming is done inside the studios, in buildings called sheds, but which look more like aircraft hangars. After the initial disappointment, its charm grew on me. Maybe this is what Hollywood looked like, anyway.

Shepperton's charm was helped by the filming going on all around, so you could brush up against anything in the canteen: men in armour, vampires out during the day, or space monsters. In 1990, while we were working on the fourth series, *Robin Hood, Prince of Thieves* was being filmed there. Although there were rumours of Kevin Costner flying in by helicopter, I never saw him. I did see a lot of his extras though, tens of muddy peasants in rags queuing in the canteen for the hotpot. It did cross my mind to mention this fact to the Salvation Army, because every down-and-out in the area could have wandered in on *Prince of Thieves* days, got a free meal, and no one would have been any the wiser. Whether they could have learnt enough convincing chatter for the queue is another matter.

'"Well," I said to him, "if you expect me to lay face down in a puddle of mud for nothing, you've got another think coming. I want another twenty quid."'

And quite right too.

Robert and I seemed to drive Craig to and from Shepperton on a kind of unofficial time-share basis. Craig lived round the corner from me, and most mornings I gave him a lift to the studio. The series were filmed during October, November and December, and Craig would be waiting inside the phone box near the tube station, blowing into his hands to try and keep warm. I wasn't really allowed to stop on this bit of road, so I had to time it to make sure he'd be there before me. Otherwise I'd have to keep going round and round the one-way system. As soon as he saw me, he'd rush out of the phone box and jump in the car, expecting it to be warmer. My car was twenty-three years old, and the heater would only just have started to warm up by the time we'd driven the twenty miles to Shepperton. Some mornings, he'd have a tape ready in his hand of some music he'd recorded and was desperate to play, forgetting that my car doesn't have a cassette player. Usually he'd sleep all the way there, waking up now and again to ask where we were.

Often we'd have spent forty minutes stuck in traffic,

going nowhere, and I'd have to bomb along the last bit to make sure we got there in time.

Most mornings, on this last bit of motorway, I'd hear an elaborate 'bibbing' noise and Chris would overtake us with any of the various forms of transport he owned: a Range Rover; a Land Rover; an E-type Jag; or any of his British motor-bikes from the 1940s. The possibilities seemed endless; we wouldn't have been surprised to see him go past on the Orient Express; on water-skis; or in a supermarket trolley with a Maserati engine.

One night after rehearsal I was giving Craig a lift home along with another actor, Jake Abrahams. A police siren started up right behind us and the car was filled with the reflection of the blue flashing light. I stopped by the side of the road. I heard the police car door open, the sound of boots on crunching gravel, and wound down my window in readiness for his face to appear.

'Good evening, madam,' he said, peering into the car. 'Do you know why we've stopped you?'

'Ah,' I replied enthusiastically, 'it's because I was doing sixty.'

'This is a forty-miles-an-hour speed limit.'

'Yes, sorry,' I replied, 'I thought I was still in the sixty-mile . . .' I petered out as he shone the torch in at my passengers, who both gave him cheeky grins. The policeman turned back to me.

'Have you had anything to drink tonight?'

I'd been sucking horrible antiseptic sweets all day, and I thought maybe he could smell them on my breath. 'It's cough sweets!' I exclaimed cheerfully.

He asked me to step out of the car. 'Would you blow into this please?' He handed me a thin black digital piece of apparatus with what looked like an aerial sticking out of it.

'It's your radio,' I replied.

'No, it's a breathalyser, would you blow into it please?'

'I thought they were like little plastic bags.'

'Not any more, madam. Would you please blow into it.'

I blew into the aerial-type thing. It showed green. 'I haven't drunk anything at all,' I added helpfully.

He started to wander around the car.

The other policeman got out of his car. He walked briskly over, came right up close to me and looked into my face. 'It is!' he exclaimed. 'It's Holly!'

'Yes,' I said. 'Hallo.'

His colleague rushed back round and stared at me blankly. The younger policeman looked into the car and shone his torch into the passenger seat. 'It's Lister!' he yelled excitedly.

'Hallo, mate,' said Craig Charles, and he started to get out of the car.

The policeman bent down to shine the torch through the rear side window. 'Well, who's in here then?' he asked.

'It's Jake. He's another Lister. I've got a double this week.'

Jake waved.

'Wow, I don't believe it!' the policeman went on, shaking his head. 'Two Listers and a Holly.' He walked back towards me. 'Well, if you can handle a spaceship, I reckon you can drive this old banger.' He thumped the roof of my car and started to walk back to the police car. 'Off you go.'

I often used to get chatting with the guest stars, who were maybe waiting around to rehearse one particular scene. Maggie Steed, who played the mad professor in the 'Quarantine' episode, was on set with us while a new version of *Wuthering Heights* was being filmed at the studios. One day we'd gone to the canteen together. I had my head down guzzling my way through a plate of particularly juicy spare ribs, when I heard her say, 'There's Ralph!'

I glanced up from my gorging to see Ralph Fiennes, cup of tea in hand, looking around the tables for somewhere to sit. He was a vision of the ultimately handsome Heathcliff, with long wild black hair.

'Ralph!' she called out in that wonderful voice properly trained actresses have.

He looked over at us. 'Maggie!' he cried, and headed straight towards her.

This called for panic stations. I hastily thrust my plate of spare ribs on to the table behind, and tried to wipe the barbecue sauce off my face with my arm. This meant that whatever lipstick I still had on was now spread around my lower face, but at the time I thought I'd got away with it. He arrived at the table. Maggie stood up and he gave her a hug. I took advantage of these vital few seconds and hastily stuck my face into my handbag to put on some more lipstick.

'Do you know Hattie?'

Don't be daft, of course he didn't.

'Hallo,' I said.

I looked into his stunning blue eyes as he sat down opposite me. It was lucky I was already sitting down, because my legs had turned to wobbly raspberry jelly. I stared at him, thinking what to say, while he and Maggie chatted excitedly. They stopped for a moment.

'Are you any relation to the explorer, Ranulph Fiennes?' I asked.

I think he said they were cousins, but I can't be sure. I was just so relieved the question had not turned out to be as stupid as it could have been. So far so good.

There was a scraping-of-chair noise, and the burly man from the table behind appeared. 'I think this is yours,' he said to me, dumping a plate of congealed meat and bones next to me on the table.

A bit of a conversation stopper, that one. For me, anyway.

Not all the guest stars on *Red Dwarf* were even human. Over the series I met a fluffy white rabbit, a tarantula and a python. Luckily I don't have a fear of fluffy white rabbits. The tarantula for the 'Demons and Angels' episode was so large I couldn't take it seriously as a spider. I could only get anywhere near it by fooling myself that it was a Scottie dog. I knew that pythons felt like soft leather and not the wet slimy creatures people dread them to be, because I'd met one before when I was a temp at an advertising company. They kept a fifteen-foot python in a glass case in reception, near to where I sat. It seemed cruel, for both of us. While I was there, a man came to feed it raw meat, and take it for a run round his neck and legs. Then, since I offered, he placed the snake around me. A receptionist of a media company, wrapped up in a python, was easily the sort of thing that could have caught on in the heady eighties.

The advantage of Shepperton was that we actually rehearsed around the sets. If Holly was to be shown on the screen, in the background of a scene, I'd stand in that position in rehearsals. This meant I would know the position of everybody else, so on camera I could pretend to look directly at the others and react to what they were saying. I'd draw little stick people on my script, so I'd remember where they were standing. Call it professionalism, call it enthusiasm, call it padding out your part. In theory, at rehearsals I could have called out my lines from anywhere around the studio, but I felt more a part of the show if I physically stood in the scene. It also reminded the rest of the cast where my lines were in the general scheme of things.

Rob and Doug were pretty open to suggestion regarding the script, although obviously they had the last say on anything. Now and then, I would suggest bits for Holly if I thought it was logical, or if I felt she'd been left out. In 'The Last Day', Holly didn't originally give Kryten a leaving present like the others, and in 'Dimension Jump' Holly didn't originally meet the debonair Ace Rimmer. Since she wasn't in the latter part of the episode, I suggested that maybe she could meet Ace, faint, then stay unconscious. Rob and Doug agreed, and while the additions didn't move the plot along to any high degree I felt happier that Holly was included.

To film Holly they used the same method as they had with Norman, and I wore the black polo-neck jumper. In addition, I had a length of thick foam rubber round my neck, covered in black material, to make sure I kept my head in the right position. It wasn't uncomfortable, but I felt like someone who'd been in a car crash and had to wear a neck brace. I would sit in front of three flats (for the benefit of non-theatricals, like myself, not a housing estate, but three sections of frame covered with black felt). The effect on camera of the black background and black polo-neck jumper was that only my face and hair would be seen on screen.

There would be a light shining down on to me, and two lights on stands, slightly to the left and right, in front of me. These would be organized by the Lighting Director, John Pomphrey, a gentleman who would walk around talking into a walkie-talkie and looking upwards, as if he had a direct line to God. I could never see anyone up there myself and had to take it on trust that his colleague really did exist, moving about the lights and scaffolding in a mysterious way. This other lighting man's name was Dai, and I used to wonder how disturbing it was for him, to be fifty foot up in the air, perched precariously on a ledge with someone on the ground shouting, 'Die! Die!'

A microphone on a stand would be placed as close to my face as possible without being in shot. Straight in front of me was a camera, and behind that, obviously, a cameraman who, on realizing he was filming a person who wasn't going to move for a couple of hours, would go off and bring himself back a seat. We would sit there, eyeball to eyeball, but for the camera in between.

A television monitor would have to be wheeled on a trolley to somewhere I could see it, among all this equipment, so I could watch the rest of the cast in their part of the studio. I could follow the action on this television, until just before my bit, when I would have to look straight into the camera and say my lines. By the wonders of technology, I would be filmed and simultaneously shown on screen in the main scene.

Although I only needed to wear a jumper that was black, I used to deck myself out totally in black; tights, shoes, skirt and sometimes even down to black cotton gloves. It helped me to feel that I was definitely in costume, and not just nipping out to the shops on a slightly chilly day. Howard, the costume designer, was always pleased if the script gave him an idea for an accessory to Holly's costume, like earrings, or a tiara, a fishing hat or a hood. The girls in the make-up department were always pleased too when I had to have my hair done differently, like slicked back or curled up, rather than my normal bob. We even got a review for series IV that said, 'Holly's hair is now far too long for a computer.' This made us wonder what length hair a computer should have.

As *Red Dwarf* progressed through the years the studio audience was made up more and more of dedicated fans – people who had not only sent off for tickets but had queued, cajoled, begged and gate-crashed for them. There was even talk of ticket touts outside the studio gates. Most sitcoms that last half an hour on television take about two-and-a-half hours to film with the studio audience. That does not include any scenes shot on location previously, which are shown to the studio audience on television monitors hanging from the ceiling. Some of the *Red Dwarf* scenes – for example, shots of model spaceships; or cute, fluffy obstinate little animals; or huge monsters worked with levers – may last ten seconds in the programme but could have taken a whole day to film. Any scenes involving explosions or fire and brimstone would, of course, be recorded beforehand. However dedicated the fans, it would not have been fair to keep them captive for weeks on end, or make them risk life and limb. Though I'm sure some of them wouldn't have minded.

Of course, in a sense, there were two crews on *Red Dwarf*. There was the crew of the *Red Dwarf* mining ship, and then there was the thirty or forty crew on the programme *Red Dwarf*, dealing with lighting, cameras, sound and everything else. Sometimes, on other shows, there can be a definite let's-get-this-over-with-then-we-can-go-home type of attitude. After all, it's a technical job and the novelty can wear off very quickly. But the crew on *Red Dwarf* were as excited about the show as anyone else. They wore the T-shirts, and there was a great atmosphere throughout all the series. They would even laugh during the tech-run, when their heads were meant to be full of thoughts about wattage and lengths of cable. On the studio day, the crew would be in early and testing out equipment. One or two of them would have to stand in front of the camera, in place of the actor, to make sure the lighting or sound would be right for later on. While some would look a bit self-conscious doing this, others became a bit stage-struck by this supporting role. Sometimes they would be well into their Cat or Lister impression when Danny or Craig would arrive and take the mickey out of them mercilessly. Often a burly member of the crew might come up to me later in the day and say proudly, 'I was you this morning!'

46. Romania

Romania was a country very much in the news during 1990. President Ceauşescu had been overthrown the year before, and a lot of problems were newly coming to light. There were news items on rioting and strikes, documentaries on ecological disasters, and individuals were inspired to drive lorry-loads of food and provisions to orphanages throughout the country. Even the Comedy Store had set up a charity, to train nurses for a children's hospital in Transylvania, in the north of Romania. There was a *Challenge Anneka* TV programme where volunteers totally renovated and refurbished an orphanage within a couple of days, providing toys and equipment. Anneka proudly showed the cameras the work that had been done, and the goods that had been sent. As she walked past some shelves in the kitchen, she spotted a china tea set, decorated with Beatrix Potter characters. 'I wonder how long this will be here for,' she pondered.

I didn't know where I would be for Christmas that year.

There were aunts and friends where I could go and scrounge Christmas dinner, or I could make my own attempt at burning a few pots and pans. A group from the Comedy Store charity were going out to the Romanian hospital to play with the children, hopefully without getting in the way, and they asked me if I wanted to come along. I readily agreed.

There were no flights on the day we were meant to leave because the Romanian Airline pilots were on strike. The next day there were still no flights to Bucharest, but we could get one to Budapest. Whether this was because it was on the way, or just next down the list alphabetically, wasn't clear. They assured us that the next stage of the flight would be arranged while we were on the plane.

We arrived at Budapest, went through customs, but could not get through passport control, because we needed a visa, which we didn't have because we hadn't expected to be visiting Hungary. It looked like we were about to spend Christmas in a clinically clean carpeted area between two sets of desks. The organizer of our trip demanded to see someone from the British Embassy or British Airways, or even British Gas, in fact anyone with a 'British' in it who could sort something out.

Eventually, a representative from Romanian Airlines arrived, straight from a Christmas Eve party, and got us out of no man's land and into the departure lounge. Rather than sit there for the next few hours though, Gary, a charity worker, and I wanted to have a quick look around Budapest. A Romanian man named Vlad decided to come with us.

We rushed out of the airport, and saw a taxi-driver leaning on his cab door at the front of the queue. He wore a blue cap, had more than a passing resemblance to Robert de Niro, and did not speak any English.

We made sounds and signs. A round tour of Budapest, bringing us back here in a hour. We hoped that was the message he'd eventually got from us. He seemed to have done. He drove us along the wide avenues, over bridges and alongside the river, until we arrived at a small castle. We stood on the battlements looking across the river at the white Christmas lights flickering in the water.

'Budapest,' said the taxi-driver.

'Beautiful,' we said.

He nodded.

We hadn't had much of a conversation with him.

'Beautiful,' he repeated.

Maybe he could understand a little English.

'Do you know Robert de Niro?' I asked him.

'Robert . . . ?'

'Robert de Niro,' I said, slowly.

'No,' he replied.

Maybe he was wary of admitting to knowing anybody to Westerners.

'You look like him,' I said, making hopefully appropriate hand gestures in the facial area. He shrugged a Robert de Niro shrug. He understood, but didn't know who I was talking about. 'Big American film star,' I announced.

He smiled a Robert de Niro smile. 'Yes?' he nodded, smiled again and shrugged.

He didn't ask if I was looking at him.

Back at the airport, the Romanian Airlines man had reappeared and had managed to sort out a train for us.

'A plane?'

No, it was definitely a train.

On Christmas Eve night, we began the twelve-hour train journey to the hospital in Transylvania. This was much more exciting than the plane. Our organizer started up the carol singing and, wrapped in nearly all the clothing from our suitcases, we worked our way through the duty-free. I'd given mine to the airline rep.

It was Christmas morning. After we'd been awake a couple of hours, the train slowly passed through Copsa Mica, a dangerously polluted town I had seen on one of the recent documentaries on Romania. Thick black smoke belched from tall chimneys in the morning twilight, and small children in buttoned-up coats and bobble-hats waved to the train from the top of a heap of black waste. The smoke and smell seeped through the closed windows and lingered for the rest of the journey.

None of us were sure of what to expect at the hospital, but thankfully it was nothing like the nightmare orphanages we'd all seen on the news. Many of the children there had come from these places and, when well enough again, would unfortunately return to them. Being in this hospital, with its clean surroundings and new playroom, may well have been the highlight of their lives so far.

During the 1980s, it had been policy to give blood transfusions to malnourished children to build them up. Any infection in this blood was passed on, because it was untested, and the needles were used over and over again.

This hospital had a ward full of babies suffering from Aids. It's a bit unnerving to say the least when a toddler's only words are 'Mama' and 'injection'. It's worse still when their favourite game is trying to jab you in the backside with an old syringe. This particular little toddler became my favourite; he'd sit on my hip and cling round my neck for the whole day, calling me 'Mama.'

We had taken packets of balloons, and the children had never seen these before. They loved them, hugged them – and quickly learnt that they burst if you tried to inject them. As far as our modest aims were concerned we hadn't done too badly. We had played with the children for a week, but we had got in the way, causing total mayhem as they ran up and down corridors, chasing balloons for the first time ever.

On the last evening, we were invited round to the flat of a Romanian couple, who had worked as volunteers. Apparently, they had done some of the refurbishment at the orphanage featured in the *Challenge Anneka* programme.

'Would you like some coffee?' asked the man.

'We have Nescafé,' the woman told us proudly.

'That would be great,' we said.

The man told us about the work he'd done, while his wife went out into the kitchen. She returned with a tray of small cups with matching saucers, decorated with Beatrix Potter characters.

I picked up the china cup and saucer. 'These are nice!' I said.

'Yes,' he said proudly, 'they came from England.'

'Yes,' I said, 'I think I've seen them on the television.'

A perk of the job, I suppose. A bone-china tea set wouldn't have lasted five minutes at the orphanage anyway. At least our group hadn't pilfered Peter Rabbit cups that had been given to needy children. Instead we'd given them love and attention – then stolen it away again, which was far worse.

47. Red Dwarf – *The Last Day*

After a show is recorded, the first time the cast see it is when everyone else sees it on the television. I had always assumed that performers would get to see any show they were in beforehand, but you soon realize how impractical and ill-advised this would be. I liked watching *Red Dwarf* the night it was actually on TV, because I knew there were five or six million other people laughing at the same bits I was laughing at.

There was usually a gap of about a year or so between the recording of each *Red Dwarf* series, and there was always a feeling of apprehension about whether or not there would be another one.

In October 1992, a few months after I was told there would be a sixth series, Rob and Doug asked me into their office for a chat. They wanted to talk about the part of Holly. There had been less of a role for her during series V, and they had been talking about some kind of change. Of course, I was hoping that this would lead to a bigger part, and met up with them in quite an excited mood. But they were rather more subdued.

'We've got something not very nice to say,' they said.

I still didn't twig immediately.

When I was a kid, playing round at this other girl's house, her parents used to ask me, 'Won't your mother be wondering where you are?'

'No,' I'd say, 'she knows I'm here.'

Rob and Doug had decided not to include the character in series VI, as there would be a change of story-line and no real role for her any more.

'Have you definitely decided?' I asked.

'Yes, we have really.'

I don't know, do you finish your coffee in these situations, or do you just leave it?

48. *Fruit Surprise*

It is a breezy Thursday in October 1994, just about lunch-time. I am sitting in the back of a brand-new black Ford Scorpio. In the front are Lee Evans and our tour manager, Grazio. We are travelling between our last gig in Preston, Lancashire, to our next gig in Aberystwyth, on the fifth day of a 33-night tour.

The ONE MILE sign for motorway services loomed up fast.

'Cup of tea anybody?' asks Grazio.

'Yes!' I said. 'We haven't been in this one!'

We pulled into a parking space as close to the entrance as possible.

'Shop! shop! shop!' we cried in mock excitement,

heading towards yet another identical bargain store where we could look at plastic flowers, stuffed toys and tins of Highland toffee. We wandered into the self-service restaurant where only the shock of the prices can snap you out of your zombie-like wandering between counters.

Touring around, it is very easy to eat the wrong food at the wrong time in the wrong place. Here was a chance to have some healthy food. On one counter, at the front of the display, was a pyramid of Knickerbocker Glory glasses, towering over bowls of various fresh-fruit salads. I took a glass and ladled in the pineapple, grapes, peach and straw-berries, carefully avoiding the unpeeled slices of red apple they use as bulk, like polystyrene packing. I found Graz and Lee tucking into egg, chips and beans. I'd rather have had that, I thought, but at least I'll have the satisfaction of knowing this vase of fruit was much better for me.

A few more miles down the road, and I didn't feel too wonderful.

'Grazio,' I said calmly, 'if you get a chance, can you pull on to the hard shoulder because . . .'

Whoosh! A jet exploded into the air like a lucky strike in a Texan oilfield. A fountain of fruit surged over the top of Lee's headrest, catching Grazio with the ricochet. He turned round, in time to see the next pineapple surge heading his way. He quickly swerved from the fast lane, across the motorway, and on to the hard shoulder. The car stopped, I opened the door and hung my head out. Lee and Graz both leapt out of the car, making high-pitched squeaking noises, and shaking pieces of fruit out of their hair.

'Sorry,' I kept trying to say, between each avalanche. The car looked like a fruit and veg market at the end of a day's trading. In the back, the floor, the seat, the ashtrays, the pocket down the side of the door where we kept the maps, all were awash with pineapple chunks. The newspapers we'd just bought to read, we used to dry out the seats and clean out the car.

'I'm sorry, leave it, I'll do it,' I whimpered.

'No, come on, we can get the worst of it done,' said Grazio gallantly, as he turned towards the front of the car and secretly retched.

'No, come on, mate, don't worry, it could happen to any of us,' said Lee.

We cleaned the car as best we could, then got back in to make our way to the next services. The two of them kept looking round at me, checking that nothing else was heading in their direction. I wiped my face, and put on some more make-up. One has to keep up appearances, after all. We pulled into the services, as close to the toilets as possible, and Grazio got my suitcase out of the boot so I could get changed. I came out to see them still cleaning the car, and Lee being asked for his autograph in the middle of wiping reconstituted fruit off the back seat. It was the best we could do for the moment, we put paper towels along the back of the seat and, with all the windows wide open, carried on our way to Aberystwyth. As I lay in the back of the car, the hills and valleys and winding Welsh lanes seemed to go on for ever.

Eventually, we approached our destination. All we had to do now was find this country hotel.

'Is the map in the back there?' asked Grazio. I looked in the pocket in the door.

'Yes, it is, but you won't want it.'

'It's all right,' he said, ever calm, 'we've got the phone number, I'll give them a ring.' He picked up his mobile from down by his seat. We all groaned. Graz wiped it as best he could and, at arm's length, tried to hear directions from the hotel receptionist.

Addison, our promoter, thought it would be best if Lee did the whole show, rather than risk me giving my impression of a blender without the lid on. The next day I felt totally fine, and we made our way to a gig in Birmingham. As soon as we arrived, I offered to take the relevant clothes to the dry-cleaners, for the two-hour service.

The next morning, Grazio got the car washed and disinfected in an attempt to get rid of the smell, something he would attempt without success for the rest of the tour. I went back to the cleaners. It was twelve-thirty, but the clothes still weren't ready. I started moaning that a two-hour service obviously didn't mean two consecutive hours. The woman, in a strong Birmingham accent, announced to a crowded shop, 'Well, actually, we're trying to get rid of the smell of vomit.'

'Thank you, that's fine,' I said, 'take your time.'

49. *Fandom*

'What, do they have, like *Star Trek* conventions and all that sort of stuff?'

'Yes, well they're *Red Dwarf*, not *Star Trek*, but yes they do.'

'Those people are mad, aren't they?'

'Well, only in a nice way.'

If half a dozen *Red Dwarf* fans get together round someone's house and watch the show on video, then this is not usually termed a convention. If they form a committee; book every function room in a four-star hotel for three days, six months in advance; organize members of the cast and crew to go there; and sell entrance tickets to a few hundred people, then this usually is. I went to the first *Red Dwarf* convention in 1992, and Dimension Jump, as it was called, has been held every year since. It is organized by the *Red Dwarf* Fan Club and is open to anyone who wants to go, although some interest in the programme would be advisable, since that is the main topic of conversation. Most of the cast turn up, along with the writers, and sometimes members of the crew or production team. Although they actually appeared in the programme, often it's the cast who leave at the end of the weekend knowing more than when they arrived.

We'd had a bit of practice at meeting the fans, as the cast would often go with Rob and Doug to their book-signings, where we would all sit in a row, and the fans would all queue up in a line for our autographs. The idea, obviously, was to encourage sales of the new book, but fans would bring every item they possessed to get a signature on it. These were fun, but by the end of the day, maybe six hours later, either our arms would drop off, or we'd forget what our names were.

I've also been a guest at other conventions in Australia, the USA and in Canada. These were each for fans of various space or comedy shows, including *Blake's 7*, *Babylon 5* and *Deep Space Nine*, in fact anything with a number in it. *Red Dwarf* is a relative virgin on the circuit of science fiction conventions. Those for *Star Trek* are very big business, with something like ten thousand fans or more attending.

The next biggest general science fiction convention, attracting about fifteen hundred people, is called Visions and is held annually in Chicago. The organizers of all these conventions are volunteers who devote pretty much most of the year to sorting everything out. As the size of the conventions grows, so too does the level of organization needed to fit all the events into ever-busy schedules.

Conventions have also built up around other comedy programmes and cult television shows. Such a cult exists around the sixties series *The Prisoner*, starring Patrick McGoohan. When I was a kid, we used to watch this show on Sunday evenings. Even though we liked it, we couldn't make head nor tail of it. It would especially annoy my dad, who would sit through it muttering to himself, then reach a crescendo of irritation.

'Bubbles! Bleed'n' bubbles! A load of bleed'n' rubbish!'

The only episode he liked was the last one, where skeletons sang 'Dem bones, dem bones, dem dry bones.'

My boyfriend Monty and I recently went to Portmeirion,

the fantastic magical place where *The Prisoner* was filmed. From London, the trip involved a six-hour train journey, on three different trains of decreasing size, finally getting off at a station in Wales called Penrhyndeudraeth. We'd looked this place up in the train timetable, and decided to buy tickets to Porthmadog, a place two stations further on, but infinitely easier to say through the nuclear-proof glass at Euston Station.

The conventions all have a similar pattern. The 'celebrity guests' each give a talk, answer questions or entertain for an hour or so, then sign autographs, have their photos taken with the fans, and generally hang around for as long as they can. There is usually a room where the videos are shown continuously, a merchandise room, a charity auction, a fancy-dress competition and a disco. Being a celebrity guest, and spending maybe four days talking to people, having your photo taken and kissing babies, can feel as if you are running for office at the next election. But it is only in this role that I've been to a convention. In fact I didn't even think I liked science fiction. I'd always thought of it as an oh-what-fun-it-will-be-when-we-have-jet-propelled-shoes view of the future. Now I realize it's more pessimistic, I'm happier. The conventions are an opportunity to meet other guests and the fans.

One *Red Dwarf* fan had gone through intensive questioning at airport security to get to the Chicago convention, because he was determined to carry a broken television with him on the plane. However much he explained what it was for, they remained suspicious. Eventually, after a personal search in the little private room, they let him through. He was probably going to have to face the same trouble taking the television back home again to Kansas. He didn't even win the fancy-dress competition, but with his blonde wig, bright-red lipstick, and the broken television over his head, I thought he made an excellent Holly.

At the same convention, I met Terry Walsh, a stunt man who appeared in various Bond films and in *Dr Who*. When he started talking about the person who'd trained him, I realized I'd met this man in a pub theatre in London. I'd gone to see a friend in a play, and during the interval a man about five foot tall, dressed quite trendily and possibly in his late fifties, started talking to me at the bar. He'd been working on the continent, and he showed me some photos of himself, wearing a suit, carrying an umbrella, and standing on one leg at the top of a fifty-foot diving-board.

At the end of the play, as the audience were leaving, he winked at me and started to walk briskly out. Tripping on the top stair, he rolled head over heels all the way down to the landing, crashed against the banisters, then rolled down the rest of the stairs backwards. People gasped and rushed to help, but he got up and cheekily took a bow. He waited for me at the bottom of the stairs.

'Going for a drink?' he winked. He walked into the pub, fell up two steps, hurled himself over a barrier and, somersaulting over a table, arrived right in front of the bar. 'What would you like?' he asked.

'Yes, he was Britain's top stunt man,' Terry told me. 'He would have been in his seventies by then. Sounds like he was on the pull that night!'

★

232

After the convention in Chicago, I spent fifteen days travelling around on an Amtrak train pass. At the Chicago main station, I walked down the staircase that was filmed in *The Untouchables*, and on to a train for New Orleans.

I went for a meal in the dining-car, and sat with a couple in their late thirties.

'Where are you from?' asked the man in a slow Southern accent I'd only heard before in films.

'London, England,' I replied.

'We're from Memphis,' he said.

'We went to Europe once,' said the woman. 'It was dirty.'

A few hours later the train slowed down as we passed nearly a mile of rubbish-tip and scrap-yard, then pulled into Memphis Station.

Working out where to go on this trip had taken me the whole seven-hour flight to Chicago. First, you have to choose a rough direction. Since it was November, I chose as far south as possible. Now you have to study the train timetable, to see where it's possible to go, because not every city in the US has a train station. You can look at the route, but it's not yet worth looking at the guidebook because there is no point choosing a place only to find you arrive downtown at two in the morning. So, to recap – you've knocked out places that don't have a train station, now you knock out places where the train stops at an unsafe hour. Only now is it worth turning to the guidebook, to see which of the places left are worth stopping at for at least one night. Since there's not a train every day, you could get off somewhere on a whim, and be stuck there for the next four days. When it came to it, there were about half a dozen places I could go to.

The first of these was New Orleans, where I could either spend a night or four days. If I spent four days, then I wouldn't have time to get to the other places across on the West Coast, so I stayed there exactly twelve hours. In that time I managed to arrive back at my picturesque hotel on foot; in a taxi; on a vintage bus; and with a horse and carriage.

'I'm going to miss you, lady,' said the porter when I left. 'I never know what you're going to turn up in next.'

I'd also gone into a restaurant and, instead of a menu, thought I'd been given the Carpenters' back catalogue. 'Jambalaya. Crawfish pie. Filet gumbo.'

My next train journey was across to Los Angeles, three days non-stop, as all the other places in between were eliminated for one reason or another when the guidebook/ timetable ruling was applied. On this journey, it seemed a good idea to book a sleeping compartment. A comfy armchair, by day, was transformed by the porter into a bed at night. I lay there looking out on to a wide-screen moving picture of the desert. Three huge meals a day were included in this sleeper ticket, and these were served in the dining-car by men in pure white uniforms with gold braid. During my visit to the USA I kept meeting Americans who had never been on a train, and I started a one-woman mission. 'They're brilliant, you've got to go on the train,' I'd say.

After a few days in LA, the next train I got was to Las Vegas, and I hated this plastic place on sight. The first hotel I stayed in had an Egyptian theme to it, with a boat ride on a plastic ancient Egyptian barge on a waterway, built around the huge foyer.

'Where does the boat trip start?' I asked the girl at reception.

'No, you mean the Nile River Cruise,' she corrected me.

'No, that's in Egypt,' I said, 'I mean the boat trip around the foyer.'

I moved out of this hotel to one that had an erupting volcano, a waterfall, real white tigers, a forty-foot fish tank and a rainforest, all before you even got to reception. I don't know what happened, but I totally changed my mind about Las Vegas and decided I loved the place.

In America, *Red Dwarf* is mainly shown on Public Service Broadcasting, and these television stations run on donations and subscriptions from their viewers. As I'd found my way to California, I helped out on a fund-raising night on a TV station where they were showing a whole night of *Red Dwarf* episodes. The head of the TV station gave me his business card; there was his name, there were all the details, and there was his title 'President'. Then he smiled, opened his wallet, and gave me another business card. 'This is my special card,' he said. It looked the same; there was his name, all the details, but with a title from 'Quarantine', 'King of the Potato People'.

A convention is a fantasy land for the guests as well as the fans, though they shouldn't let the fame and attention they receive there go to their heads. In Canada, Robin Curtis, an actress from *Star Trek*, and myself had spent four days at a convention, signing autographs. We went out for a wander around Halifax and were leaning, looking at our street map, when a man came over to us.

'Excuse me –' he said.

'Yes, of course,' we said, each diving for a pen in our handbag to sign his autograph book.

'Excuse me,' he continued, 'could you not lean on my car?'

Because I used to collect autographs myself, I often look through people's books when they give them to me. Quite often a lot of kids have been to Disneyland, and to sign your name after 'Goofy' kind of puts the whole thing into perspective somehow.

50. *Epilogue*

In March 1996, I performed my hour stand-up show for two weeks at the very first Adelaide Comedy Festival.

After the festival, I travelled around for a few weeks, and went up to Queensland to see the world's oldest rainforest.

My friend, Gretta, was in Australia, so we met up and got the bus to Ayers Rock. We arrived in the late afternoon, and saw a man in a leather jacket standing in the street, giving out leaflets.

'We've got to do this,' I said.

As we rode alongside Ayers Rock at sunset, swigging champagne on the back of a Harley-Davidson being driven by an Alice Springs Hell's angel, I could imagine that maybe I was Born to be Wild.